A Cow's Tail for a Compass

A Cow's Tail for a Compass

Cowboy Poetry and Short Stories

by Leon Flick

JUNIPER PRESS

A Cow's Tail for a Compass
Copyright © 2000
by Leon Flick

Juniper Press
Box 6
Plush, OR 97637

ISBN 0-9701448-0-6 (cloth)

ISBN 0-9701448-1-4 (pbk.)

Library of Congress Catalog Card Number
00-191967

Book and cover design by Patricia Broersma
Cover art by Leon Flick

Manufactured in the United States of America

DEDICATION

This book is dedicated to all the characters in
this book who, by being human,
have given it its source.

Also to any one who has spent his life using a
cow's tail for a compass.

TABLE OF CONTENTS

ABOUT THE AUTHOR

Born to Carroll and Vivian Flick on March 4, 1954, Leon entered the scene behind two sisters, Thelma and Nancy. As a three year old, the family moved from his birthplace of Gunnison, Colorado, to Lakeview, Oregon. There, he grew up on working ranches. He learned to ride on Chief, an old paint horse that was about 16 hands high. Chief, God rest his soul, had been teacher, friend, baby sitter, and loyal companion to several kids, and was worth twice his weight in gold. Leon is still reminded of that old friend every time he sees some little guy crawlin' up some horses leg, swingin' on the saddle strings, finally gettin' a stirrup, and climbin' into the saddle. The world is a big place when you're a "button," and God never made a better place to view it from than the back of a horse.

Leon and his wife, Billie, live in Plush, Oregon, a small, high desert town of 60 people about 40 miles north of where California and Nevada join Oregon. Remote would be a fitting word, as it is over 200 miles to even the nearest freeway. It's filled with sagebrush, rocks, cows, and a very few of the nicest families on Earth.

Leon started sharing his poetry and stories in 1988 at Elko, Nevada, and has entertained people in 13 Western states. Other than his entertaining, a little guiding and fencing, Leon and Billie still make their living using a cow's tail for a compass.

FOREWORD

I've been acquainted with Leon Flick since he was in school, going to junior and high school rodeos. He wasn't much more than a kid when he went to work for Phil Lynch running the JJ outfit in Warner Valley.

I never worked with Leon except branding calves or maybe helping some outfit ship, but I noticed that he seemd to wind up in the right place more often than not, which is about all any of us try to accomplish on our better days. I did work close enough to Leon that our horse tracks crossed occasionally, and whenever his name came up around the fire at night it seemed like whatever you heard was never anything a man would have to hide from. The immediate conclusion you drew was that his peers considered him a cowboy. That is about as good a compliment as one man a-horseback ever pays to one another.

I kind of lost track of Leon for a few years. That was about the time he left Plush to see how people in other parts of the West work cattle from the back of a horse.

The next time we ran into one another, he had moved back to the Warner Valley area and was working in double harness with his better half, Billie. Billie is not only a likable attractive young lady, but is also about as good a hand around livestock as anyone going down the road. If you are out somewhere and get yourself into a jackpot, you can be sure that there is help close at hand if she is anywhere nearby. The two work together most of the time and are so much in demand around their part of the world that they have a tough time getting enough time off to do their grocery shopping.

When Leon cracked out at his first poetry gathering in Elko, Nevada, the stuff he was writing about was so authentic and well-written that he was almost immediately accepted as one of the better cowboy poets in the movement. He and I have spent many hours since then traveling down the road to poetry gatherings throughout the West.

I'm not going to spend a lot of time praising Leon's poetry because it will be pretty obvious what it's like when you read this book. You will find not only some excellent verse but several anecdotes that will amuse and entertain you, especially if you have a little buckaroo in your soul. It will be clear that he writes about things he has lived and that are dear to his heart. Leon Flick loves his chosen profession! Leon Flick is a cowboy!

—Sunny Hancock

A Cow's Tail for a Compass

DAYS

Have you ever seen it rain so hard,
 it soaked your underwear?
Or seen the wind blow so damned hard,
 you thought your skin would tear?
Or been so parched for want of drink,
 you thought that you might die?
Or been so mad at everything,
 you'd want to sit and cry?
Have you been so cold your hands turned blue,
 and zippers would not close?
With hands and gloves and coat so wet,
 you couldn't wipe your nose?
Or seen the dust so dry and thick,
 you couldn't get your air?
Or tried your best to do things right
 for them that didn't care?
Well, maybe you're a cowboy.
 These extremities do exist.
But it's all the days that lay between
 that cowboys like the best.

THE BADGER WALTZ

The old man was gettin' fairly long in the tooth, but he wasn't plumb down yet. He didn't do too much around the place anymore but putt around the little field by the house and keep it irrigated. This was good for the old feller because it gave him something to do that meant something. Every morning, you'd see him shuffle down the ditch bank with his shovel, all decked out in the same bib-overalls, like he'd worn most of his life.

On one particular morning, he saw a badger go into one of the four foot long culverts that let water out of the main ditch and in the field. The old gentleman's shuffle increased to a medium shuffle, a gait we hadn't seen him use in quite a while.

When he reached the spot, ole mister badger stuck his nose out of the end of the culvert to check things out. Grandpa unloads a load of shovel right at the end of it. The badger seemed to have the edge when it came to reflexes, but not to patience.

Now patience is not one of a badger's more superior qualities, and although the badger did play along with the old gentleman quite a while, after about ten trips from one end of the culvert to the other, ole mister badger had had enough.

When Grandad swung his shovel this time and shuffled off to the other end of the culvert, Mister Badger came out the same end that he'd just left and was in hot pursuit. He didn't have any trouble overtaking the old man and gettin' ahold of the bottom of those bib-overalls.

It was quite a sight to see. This old gentleman and this badger, dancin' all around the pasture. The badger was backing up and growling, and Grandad was swingin' his shovel like Mickey Mantel. His shins got pretty chewed up, but it was all from the shovel. He finally got one landed square on the badger's lid, and the dance was over. Every since then, we've referred to it as "The Badger Waltz."

MY PLACE

A city feller asked me, "How big a place had I?"
You see, I'd never owned a place,
and I didn't want to lie.
So I used this for an answer,
and I'd given it some thought.
"It's pretty big," I told him.
"If you'd cross it at a trot,
well, it'd take you quite a little while.
For God, He was the maker.
You see on my place mister,
well, it covers lots of acres.

"I was born in Colorado,
and I lived there 'till I's three.
Dad worked in Taylor Basin.
That was my first place, you see.

"Then dad took a leave from cattle life,
and we moved farther West.
Out to Southern Oregon,
where he mined and let cows rest.

"But, mining didn't suit him,
so in a couple years,
we're back to runnin' cattle.
Some cows and calves and steers.

"Now, I'm right at six years old now,
and it's there I learned to ride.
I'm kind of in the drag yet,
Not too much up on either side.
But I guess on this place, mister,
is where I did my growin'.
I was fifteen when we left that place.
There's lots that I'm not knowin'.

"But I've learned enough to be some help,
Not always in the way.
Before Dad leased the next place,
he asked if I might stay,
And we'd run it like the family place
that it had been for years.
while the owner's son finished college.

Then he'd be taking over there.
I guess on this place, mister,
I became a buckaroo.
We had lots of 'outside country,'
and room to trot there, too.
I really did enjoy it there:
I'd a stayed there 'till I died. Although,
the son is home from college,
so it's time for us to go.

"I guess I left the nest then
and was out there on my own.
Though Mom still did my laundry
and let me use the phone.

"I helped 'em gather cattle, camped,
and worked the summer seasons.
Then I wandered off to college.
I guess most for social reasons.

"Then I went back to workin' cattle.
On that desert I would roam,
all around that Warner Valley,
and the town of Plush that I call home.

"I worked an outfit down there,
for right at eleven years.
When circumstance 'caused my leavin',
in the catch corral, I shed tears.
For on this place, mister,
I had rode a lot of colts.
Most of 'em packin' bridles now,
and we're sharin' our last oats.

"Then I saw the great Steen's Mountain
for the first time, 'cept at distance.
And from the top of Kieger Gorge,
you still can't see the back fence.

"Then down into California,
to the 'Rancho Arroyo Seco,'
that lay a little eastward
of the city, Sacramento.

"Then back up to northern Oregon,
to a place called 'Seven Diamond.'
A cattle corporation,
that was good for stories rhymin'.

"So you ask how big my place is?
Well, you ought to know by now.
It's bigger than the world outside.
My place is horseback – with a cow."

TOM'S COPENHAGEN

We'd just split up one morning after trotting out from camp. We weren't a quarter of a mile apart yet when I saw Tommy's horse stumble in the rocks and go down pretty hard. It's always a tense moment when a horse goes down. You never know if the rider has gotten away clean, or if he's fouled or hurt and about to go for a severe dragging. Well, the horse gets up, and I can see that Tom isn't hung up, but he just stays down. He's up on his knees, with his head right on the ground, and kind of floundering around on his front end. I figure that he's hurt bad and clatter through the rocks as fast as I can and get right over there.

"You okay?" I asked.

"Yea, I'm all right," he growled.

"Well, what is it that's wrong then?" I inquired.

"Well, it's like this," he told me, "I lost my glasses, and I spilt my Copenhagen." By this time, I can see that he's scooped up what he can find of his Copenhagen and put it back into his can. He's busy picking out all of the little sticks and rocks.

"This is my last can until we make it back in. I knew that if I went and searched for my glasses and didn't find them that I'd never find my Copenhagen again either. I can make it in without my glasses, but I'd never live through the day without my Copenhagen. A feller has to pick his priorities you know."

FIRST TASTE OF LIQUOR

This poem kind of leads one to
believe that my father is a
drinking man. I don't want in
any way to imply that, because
he is not. It's just a story that I
heard and put to rhyme.

Well, I'd sat there, and I'd melted,
    in the front seat of that car.
While my papa, dear ole Papa,
    he was "barred-up" in the bar.
And I was too young
    to be by Papa's side.
So I sat in that car,
    till I guess my brain had fried.
Finally I decide,
    "This has gone long enough."
So I mustered my courage,
    and all of that stuff.
And I strode through the door
    like I owned the place.
And I felt the cold stare,
    as Dad looked in my face.
And my young voice cracked,
    as I asked if we'd go.
I could tell by the look in his eye,
    it was no.
"You young whipper-snapper,
    I'll say when we leave."
Then he winked at the "bar-keep"
    A trick up their sleeve.
And he ordered us "doubles"
    My first taste of liquor.
"Now we'll shoot 'em down,
    and I bet that I'm quicker."
So at the word go,
    we both shot 'em down.
It burned my ole belly
    and turned it around.
While I coughed and I sputtered,
    they thought it was funny.
Dad ordered another.
    He still had the money.

So the "keep" kept on pourin',
    till we had six or eight.
We were fixin' on another,
    but a little too late.
Just as Dad asked
    if we might have one more,
It's then that he "passed-out,"
    in a heap on the floor.
Well, I pushed, and I pulled,
    and I prodded and goaded.
It took all my strength,
    but at last, now he's loaded.
Then I gets in the car
    and heads her for home.
And there's no pair drunker
    from Texas to Nome.
And on the way home,
    I drift off through the timber.
Neither one of us hurt much.
    We're both pretty limber.
But when Mom got there,
    stuff hit the fan.
Dad got his tail chewed,
    and I got my tail tanned.
Dad, he's a grumblin',
    'Cuz I totaled the car.
And Mother's upset,
    'Cuz I went in the bar.
And now I sit grounded,
    and it's unjust you see.
Hell, I couldn't see over the dash.
    I just had turned three.

THE BARKEEP'S TRAP

*This poem is based on a true story that was
told to me by Everett Hilbert. It came out of the
Middle Fork of the John Day River country.*

It was in a lodge-pole thicket,
    where these steers were runnin' free.
And they had been, this would be their seventh year.
They were wild as elk and just as fast.
    I'd seen 'em lead the pack.
They could flat out-run a coyote, chasin' deer.

They had a knowledge of the woods,
    and every hole was home.
They knew the secret trails down every draw.
They knew which ridge to follow
    and every way off every rim.
These eight ole steers, the worst I ever saw.

And the feller that did own 'em,
    didn't care if they came home.
He'd wrote 'em off as gone, some time ago.
'Cuz he did his work a foot-back.
    He didn't ride a horse.
In fact, the only gear he had was "slow."

He'd putt around with his old team,
    put up a little hay,
though his cows were on the "outside" most the time.
He could walk right up and pet 'em,
    they'd eat corn out of his hand.
A hobby was his herd, a small past-time.

Except for eight ole mossy steers,
    that sought a different style.
They lived wild in country steeper than their face.
And though several hands had jumped 'em
    while ridin' out for strays,
no one yet had kept up with their pace.

But, down there at the tavern,
    which was the hub of life,
and where everybody stopped to shoot the breeze,
they had been the conversation,

over many open beers.
And everyone could catch 'em there, with ease.

Them ole steers sure burned them young bucks
        that was workin' other spreads,
'Cuz the owner'd told 'em, "Just to let 'em be."
They all swore that they could catch 'em.
        'Cuz they was salty hands.
But, the owner said, "To let them steers, run free."

Until, one day, he pulled out—
        folded up, lock-stock-and-barrel,
And he stopped there at the bar to say good-bye.
And he said, "Them eight ole mossy steers,
        I'll leave 'em for the takin'.
They belong to anyone who wants to try."

Well, this raised a many eyebrow,
        and it started up a stir.
Many palms were rubbed together there in glee.
'Cuz every salty puncher,
        that thought he was a hand,
just knew them eight ole steers belong to me.

But them steers sure proved 'em different,
        and it cost 'em lots of hide—
Even crippled up a pony now and then.
And as reputation deepened,
        outside cowboys tried their luck.
But to no avail, 'Cuz no one brought 'em in.

Then, them cowboys got to claimin'
        that them steers would all die free.
'Cuz there weren't no one could catch 'em, even one.
And the barkeep, who'd said nothing,
        kinda smiled there to hisself.
"I'll get all eight when you salty bucks are done."

Well, how they all "hoo-rahed" him.
        How they laughed until they cried.
'Cuz the barkeep, he was crippled, bent, and old.
He'd given up his cowboy life
        some twenty years before.
To save his stove-up body from the cold.

And the young bucks kept on laughin',
    'till he backed 'em in a corner
when he asked 'em if they'd care to place a bet?
He'd bet an even fifty,
    or up to next month's pay.
"'Cuz I ain't seen a hand amongst you yet."

Well, every cowboy swallowed.
    Each and every one did bite.
The worst of them, they bet their next month's pay.
And the barkeep made 'em promise,
    if they'd leave them steers alone,
he'd have 'em in just three weeks of that day.

He would do 'em even better,
    he'd lead 'em up through town.
Take a circle all around the street, and then,
he'd put 'em all together,
    and hold 'em there in back,
in his flimsy, little, run-down, milkcow pen.

Well, the boys all got to smilin',
    'Cuz they knew they couldn't lose.
And the barkeep started oilin' up his tack.
And they swore they'd leave it to him,
    That they'd leave them steers alone.
But, in three weeks time, they'd surely all be back.

"You're welcome in here any time,
    'Cuz I ain't a gonna close.
Except upon the morning of the day
when I lead them steers down main street,
    and parade 'em all around.
And fellers, don't forget to bring your pay."

You could hear the laughter echo
    as they rode off in the night.
And the thoughts of extra money starts 'em dreamin'.
And the barkeep was a grinnin',
    as he finished up his tack.
'Cuz all the summer long, he'd been a schemin'.

And he'd slipped away, in his spare time,
    and built a mighty trap

that lay in a thicket made of lodge-pole pine.
And he knew that it would hold 'em.
       Of this, he was quite sure.
'Cuz in his day, he'd handled wild bovine.

And the barkeep left that very night
       with all that he would need.
His milkcow, in the moonlight, led behind.
And the cowbell, that he'd ordered,
       he had hung around her neck.
And he thought of extra money when it chimed.

And in the trap, he grained her,
       Every night and every morn.
And no one even knew that he was gone.
Then he'd turn her loose, throughout the day,
       so she could roam around.
He was hopin' that it wouldn't take too long

'til those wild steers threw in with her.
       With no one there to bother,
wouldn't be too long until they knew her bell.
Within a week, by signs of beds,
       just outside the trap,
he knew his plan was working very well.

Then at night, he'd tie his cow up
       and leave the gate ajar.
In the trap, he placed some salt and extra corn.
And he knew his time was comin'
       and that everything was right
when he saw the steers were in the trap one morn.

But he sat 'em out and waited,
       'till they finally went to water.
'Cuz he knew if he was spotted, he was done.
Then he grained and turned his cow out,
       But he came back before dark
and hid up in a tree to watch the fun.

That night the milkcow came in
       for to eat her nightly meal.
Wasn't long before the steers followed behind.
And when all eight steers had entered,

he gently shut the trap
with a rope that was connected to his blind.

Now the easy part was over,
        and the hard part, it began.
As he roped each steer and tied him to a tree.
Then he heeled each steer and stretched him out
        and layed him on the ground,
sewed their eyelids shut, so each steer couldn't see.

And with five days left to work with,
        he set his herd go free.
It was rabid, mad, confusion, at it's best.
And they trashed 'bout half that thicket,
        'fore they wouldn't trust their feet.
Confused and winded, they soon stopped to rest.

And in their total darkness,
        and in their total fear,
acute now was their hearing and their smell.
And the only thing they trusted,
        and that gave a sprig of hope,
was the ringin' of that milkcow and her bell.

And they soon all gathered to it,
        and they stuck to her like glue.
She'd lead 'em down to water and to feed.
And they learned to stay right with her,
        and they followed were she went.
She was the eyes that every steer did need.

And on the morning of the day,
        the barkeep led her in.
Took his circle all around the street and then,
he put them all together,
        and he held 'em there in back.
In his flimsy, little, run-down, milkcow pen.

And the cowboys watched with saggin' jaws
        and disbelievin' eyes.
With their dreams of extra money up in smoke.
And the barkeep said he'd buy the drinks
        while they evened up the score.
And the worst of them, they knew, they were flat broke.

But the barkeep didn't skin 'em,
    said he'd leave no man flat broke.
They could pay him off a little at a time.
But he hung the bell above the door,
    a hangin' on a string.
To remind 'em, every time, they heard it chime.

HERBIE'S HOBBLES

I was lookin' for a job one time and told a friend of mine that was selling for Walco at the time, to keep his ears open. It wasn't too long before I got a call. It was from a ranch up in northern Oregon, that ran about 2500 mother cows and about 3000 yearlings. I knew the cowboss at the time, and he tells me that they take the cows down on the Columbia river in the fall and winter on corn circles and volunteer wheat.

"The weather's not bad, and we don't have to feed much hay. We are busy calving right now, and we're taggin' the calves as they are born and giving a shot of selenium. I had a guy leave last week, and the only help I have right now is our truck driver. He can catch one if he's still wet, but if he ever gets his legs under him and dried off, he's got away without a shot or his tag. I've got another kid comin' right away, and he'll stay 'till we're done calvin', but I need a full-time man. I was wondering if you and the wife might be interested? Even if you're not thinking full-time, I could sure use somebody to finish calving these cows out and ship them home to me."

Billie and I talk it over, pull the pin, and head that direction. When we get there, the man that has just arrived, is a good friend of ours. Mark is a good hand, and lots of fun to be around. He's been there for about a week, and I ask him about the truck driver.

"Other than being pretty lazy, he tells me, he's about like two guys gone. He doesn't get out very early, but if you're lucky you can get away from him and do things by yourself. It's a lot easier that way. The boss tells me, that we're supposed to put up with him until they start shipping back home."

We had a good time that spring. The weather was a lot milder than where we had been; we got in lots of ropin', and we were having a good time on our colts. The boss was taking care of things at the home ranch, and we could run things to suit ourselves. We could trot everywhere we needed to go and were gettin' lots of miles in on those colts.

About two weeks before we started shippin' back home, we were moving baby pairs out on some grassy corners of the farm circles. The boss is there, and the truck driver is really puttin' on a show for him. He's up early every morning and talks like he's been doin' it all. It isn't very long until it comes back to haunt him.

We'd hold the cows up about noon and let them "mother-up" while someone trotted back for the trailer and lunch. When the truck driver saw the trailer, he'd trot over, tie his horse in the back, and sit in the pickup and listen to the radio. The rest of us would go in one at a time, grab a sandwich, and bring it back out to the bunch. That way, there was always at least a couple of people holdin' those baby calves from going back. One day we had a "run-back."

By the time the truck driver woke up, got his horse untied and bridled, and caught up, we had the wreck under control. Billie has gone in for a sandwich, and the boss is having a little chat with the truck driver.

"You get a pair of hobbles, and until you do, you use this little rope," the boss tells him.

He goes back over to the trailer and tells the wife, "The boss tells me that I have to get a pair of hobbles, and until I do, I have to tie my horse in the trailer with this little bitty short rope."

LISTEN TO THE SUN GO DOWN

One evening I walked out on this
rim above Plush, just to kind of
regroup and relax. It was in the
head of the JJ, just where Honey
Creek breaks out of the canyon,
and into the Warner Valley. An
oldtimer had once told me,
"Anyone can watch the sun go
down, but you have to be able to
listen to it to really enjoy it."
I believe he was right.

Upon a warm September's eve,
the sun was dipping low.
I sat myself upon a rim,
from there to watch the show.

The shadows were their longest now,
as darkness soon would be.
I closed my eyes and listened,
to the sounds I couldn't see.

The quail chatted nervously,
about to go to bed.
The hoot-owl screeched a different tune.
His whole night lay ahead.

The rock-chuck whistled one last cry,
and from his warm rock, he did slide.
The deer crept from the willows,
No longer there to hide.

The coyote howled from up on top,
before his nightly quest.
The wasps that had been buzzing
were now safe, within their nest.

The magpie and the meadowlark
and rooster pheasant too,
All said, "See you in the morning,"
and off to roost they flew.

The bobcat didn't say much
as he tested out the air.
The porcupine wandered to the creek
to get a drink from there.

The nighthawks were coming about to life
after hiding all day from the sun.
The muskrat and the beaver splashed,
either working or having fun.

And I can promise you one thing,
you'll smile instead of frown,
If you close your eyes and open your ears,
and listen to the sun go down.

I'M OUT OF HORSE

Now cowboys were just a necessary evil that you had to have as long as you wanted to run cows. Or that was the opinion of one feller that had a big outfit up in the Great Basin country.

This story was told to me by the feller that did it, so I reckon he ought to know. This is how he related it to me:

The feller that owned the outfit, hated cowboys. Especially ones wearin' big chowchills rowels in their spurs. But I needed them spurs, just to ride the horses this ole feller was throwin' under me. I finally got canned over them, but I never took them off.

It was in the fall, so we were sent over to the yearling end of the operation to help ship. The boss had called the cow boss on that end of the ranch, and said, "I'm sendin' over a couple of the cockiest little bronc riders you ever saw. Throw your worst horses at 'em and don't cut 'em any slack."

Just as luck would have it, they had just ran in a bunch of horses from the outside, so fresh horses weren't going to be a problem. Running with this bunch of horses was a nine year old gelding that had jumped out of the round corral with a saddle when he was four. He hadn't been seen again until this gather. This is the horse that they gave me the morning that we shipped.

I finally got him choked down and got a halter on him. While he's down, I just tie up a leg or two, saddle him, get my snaffle bit in his face, and was just going to come up on him. Just as I'm about ready to untie his feet, my brother brings me over this big cardboard box and says, "Here, brother Clark, take this with you." It didn't last at all for a quirt.

This ole horse comes up lookin' to tear up the world. The only thing that didn't come up off the ground was his head. After about ten minutes of the rest of the cowboys runnin' by me, tryin' to get this ole horse to quit buckin' and line out, they just left me. I figure this ole horse will buck until he just drops. We had bucked across the meadow for quite a ways, when this ole horse dives into a big bunch of willows, and just goes to suckin' air. By this time, I'm suckin' quite a bit of air myself.

About that time, the boss drives around the corner in his pickup. He stops and demands to know what the hell is going on.

"This is a hell of an outfit you run here," I said. "I'm not even a quarter of a mile away from the house, and already I'm out of horse."

Looking back, it was no wonder that he didn't like cowboys.

GOOD OLE GIRLS

*This is a poem that I wrote about my
wife, Billie. She is as good a hand as
most men that I have worked with, and
a damned sight better to sleep with.
There are a lot of other women that this
poem also applies to. Not that I have
slept with them, but they are sure a
pleasure to work cows with.*

There's some of them good ole cowgirls left.
Their long braids hang so fine.
And they can pull a snaffle bit,
and they're damned good with their twine.

They'll tangle with the biggest bull,
Either rope him or help tail him down.
They're not afraid to bump a buckin' horse
when you're about to hit the ground.

They're always in position
on a circle, long or tight.
They know what's left behind 'em,
and they'll swing both left and right.

They'll hit a long trot when you're gatherin'.
You can hear 'em yell for miles.
But they're quiet in a rodeer,
knockin' pairs out, single file.

And when you're at a brandin',
either ropin' or on the ground,
They know what needs done, and they do it.
You won't find 'em standin', lookin' around.

Be it hot and dry and dusty,
or a wind that's full of snow,
there's something about them good ole girls,
that sets my heart aglow.

THE BUCKLE

This big trophy buckle I'm wearin',
it's got quite a story to tell.
    I've wore it so long,
    the engraving is gone,
but it's still something I wouldn't sell.

And you see 'em wherever you travel.
And their owners all feel just like me.
    Reminiscin' the day,
    when they took all the pay,
from the fellers who'd all paid a fee.

It might have been won at some ropin',
when you nodded and got out just right.
    Your heeler was there
    and scooped up the pair,
and no one could beat you that night.

Or that colt that you are so proud of.
He can spin, and he'll sure watch a cow.
    He'll bury his hocks
    in the ground with no rocks.
He's one of a kind, I'd allow.

The horses that couldn't quite catch you,
The calves that you tied in a flash,
    The odds you resisted,
    Some bronc that you twisted.
The winnin'. The glory. The dash.

If you ask, you will get an accounting
of just how this buckle was won.
    Bulls dippin' so low,
    they filled your boots full.
Or some sun-fishin' son-of-a-gun.

How the crowd stood and cheered for an hour.
For they often don't see such a wreck.
    The fight was non-stop,
    but you came out on top,
Each jump with your spurs in his neck.

And stories get better, as time ages on,
as stories are sure apt to do.
  But the buckle attests,
  that you beat all the rest.
To win one, that's all that you do.

But buckles don't say who all entered,
and folks that were there'd have to scoff.
  With tremblin' knees,
  I went to the dees,
but the other two fellers, fell off.

JOHN HANGER'S MUCKING

The boss at this auction yard, and I, were about the same age, and kept things pretty lively around there. He was always calling me if there was a little work between sale days.

One time I was tending the barn, in case anyone brought in anything the day before the sale. The boss was out hauling in several little trailer loads of cattle that he had put together during the week. It was getting pretty late, and he told me that there was one more load before we called it a day. He returned in about an hour and hollers at me to set up the tagging chute.

"I've got one cow to hold back," he says. "The rest are just butcher cows. Tag 'em as they come in and put them in the butcher pen. I can hold back the cow I need on the trailer." You couldn't see back to where he was, but he said he didn't need any help.

A couple of cows come in. I tag them and put them in the butcher pen. Another cow comes in. I tag her and put her in the butcher pen. Two more drift in. I tag them and put them in the butcher pen.

All the time, you can hear quite a bit of rattling around back there. But, I just figure it's the cow that he's trying to keep on the trailer. All of a sudden, this big Charolais cow comes tearing into the tagging chute, and she sure is upset. Everything is quiet around the trailer, so I figure she's the cow that he's been trying to hold back.

"What do you want me to do with this ol' rip?" I hollers. No answer. I go back out to the trailer to see if things are all right. The boss is laying in the bottom of a pile of ripped up clothes and cow tracks. He's bleeding in a few spots and not getting much air.

"You all right?" I asked him.

He doesn't really get too much out in the way of words, but nods his head that he's not hurt too bad. I give him time to get some air.

"What happened?" I asked.

24

"That ole Charolais cow is the one I wanted to hold back," he explains, "but she was the first one off of the trailer. I didn't think she was a bit cranky when I loaded her, but she was damned sure on the fight when we got here. She caught about half of my body between the end of the trailer gate and the wall, and she's been standing there hammering on me every since. Every time she'd back off to hit me again, I'd slide down about half an inch. She never did give me time to get unpinned from behind that trailer gate. She just kept hammering. I finally slid down far enough that I got under the gate. When she got done walking on me, I managed to crawl under the trailer."

Then he added, "Put that old rip in the butcher cow pen too."

JUST LAY DOWN AND SULL UP

Another little episode that happened to John while I was working for him, happened like this:

One particular outfit up in that country ran some fairly snuffy brangus cows. I think they would catch what they could during the week and bring them to town on sale day. It seemed if they brought 18 head to town, you'd only have to make 17 sorts. There would be anything from day old calves, right on up to old gummer bulls.

This auction yard was fairly small, and most of it was covered and on concrete. This was great because it also rained a lot over on that side of Oregon. It was set up to where the cattle came off of the trucks or stock trailers and right through a tagging chute.

One sale day this outfit brought in a small load, and we were able to let them out of the tagging chute one at a time and send them right to their little pens without having to turn them into one of the sorting alleys. "Put this little bred cow in one of the 'B' pens," the boss tells me. "You'd better be right behind her to close the gate too," he cautioned.

I got outran and didn't quite get to the gate in time, and here she came. I did a quick 360 and lit out back down the alley. This ole girl is thinkin' she'd like to get me down and give me a piece of her mind.

When we reached the end of the alley, I grabbed the corner post and slid around it, taking a 90 degree turn and stopped. The heifer couldn't make the turn, slipped on the concrete and slid into the tagging chute, causing the whole barn to rattle.

The boss has since gone on to other tasks and has forgot what he's got me doing or what I'm even working with. I just happened to be face to face with him as the cow slid into the tagging chute, flat on her side.

"What's going on here?" he asks, not being the kind to allow any unnecessary roughness on the stock. "Oh, it's just like one of these brangus cows to get mad and lay down and sull up." I told him.

All of the time this cow is trying to get her feet under her so she can proceed with the little chase she's started.

"What do you mean by that?" the boss says, lookin' kind of puzzled. "Well, just look at her." I told him.

When John turned back to the cow, I was already four lengths out in front of the race. It suddenly dawned on John that he was in the race and runnin' a close second.

"Come on, Hanger. She's gonna get you." I offered back over my shoulder, laughin'.

John finally reached the fence and got about half way over, when the cow reached him and gave him that added little boost that he needed to go sailing on into the next pen.

As we lay there laughing, he says, "I couldn't figure out what you meant. 'Just get mad and lay down and sull up.'"

WET TOBBACKER

The first year of my life, or at least that
summer, was spent in a little cow camp
high in the Rocky Mountains. Taylor
Park Grazing Association was where
Dad was working at the time, and my
father was riding for the outfit out of a
cow camp they called "Tin Cup."
Lightning struck the stove pipe of our
little cabin that summer, and Mother
was eating a piece of pie off of the wood
cook stove at the time. Dad had just cut
some wood with an old crosscut saw
and had just laid it down. He said that
the blue flames shot off the teeth of that
saw and really danced around. When
he came in the cabin, Mom was sitting
over in the corner of the kitchen crying.
"Don't worry," he said,
"it didn't hit me."
"Well, by damned, it did me!"
Mom has been hit twice in her life, and I
got a pretty good shot closing a gate
later in life. But at the time,
I had other duties.

I was born in March, so I still saw a bit,
of the winter
'cuz it ain't 'till June that the sun gets lit.
Ma and Pa were camped that season,
ridin' for an association,
That threw their cows together
up there high in Taylor Basin.
Now Dad would keep the salt scattered
and the bulls from bunchin' up.
But, when a major job was called for,
all the ranchers would come up.
Now, Mom would cook for a week or two,
while the cowboys did what cowboys do.
They might have been a brandin'
or a gatherin' from afar.
And around that little cow-camp,
I'd become a quite a star,
especially to ole Rich Vader.

Every morning against his chest,
he'd pack me 'round that cabin floor
while Mom cooked breakfast for the rest.
Then one day, he ate with his coat on,
and he said that he was chilled.
But Rich and I know'd that he lied,
'cuz as he held me, I had spilled.
Then just before they mounted,
ole Rich, passed his plug around.
And, when everyone had took a chew,
he threw it on the ground.
Then he took off his coat of feathers,
'cuz it was stiflin' too hot.
And he laughed at their pain,
as he showed 'em the stain.
Then they lined out in a trot.

DRIFTERS

You see 'em now, from time to time.
They haven't got a home.
They have no friends and family.
They're always on the roam.

They never get acquainted.
They never stay that long.
It seems before they're settled in,
they're all packed up and gone.

There's some you wouldn't want around,
And others, always welcome.
No matter what the reason,
to live, some men need lonesome.

DON'T FAINT

I was helpin' move some cows down the road one morning when the school bus from Plush came through them, headed for Adel. The bus was just a Suburban, as we didn't have too many kids to transport back and forth. As the teacher was slowly making her way through the cows, she pulled up along side of one of these ole girls, and as the cow turned away from her, she kind of bumped the side of the Suburban.

When she came back through, she told me that she had bumped a cow, but said that she hadn't hurt her any. She then went on to tell me that one of the young boys riding with her had given her some pretty good advice. Young Joe put it this way.

" Dad says you really have to be careful because sometimes if you hit 'em too hard, they'll faint and never wake up."

TOGETHER AT CHRISTMAS

The wind was wild and full of snow
as it tore against our skin.
Just one more mile across the top,
And four more miles on in.
We started down the canyon.
The snow was deeper now.
But the wind had died to nothing,
and it all seemed better somehow.
We were headed to the folks for Christmas,
The pack-horse loaded down.
And the kids were cold, but happy.
They wore smiles instead of frowns,
For they knew what was in store for them—
Christmas at Gram's and Gramps.
As we made the bend, we could see the smoke
And the lights from the kerosene lamps.
An ole pot-bellied stove to warm them,
cookies and hot chocolate too.
And a big hug from Grandma and Grandpa
to set their hearts anew.
While the kids and Ma were warmin' up
and tellin' the news of the day,
Pops and I would share a joke
while puttin' the horses away.
We'd give 'em an extra bite of grain,
some timothy and wild-meadow hay.
We'd check their water, close up the barn,
and head for the house for the rest of the day—
For this was the day before Christmas,
A time of excitement and joys.
And a long wait, until in the morning,
when the kids could open their toys.
After we'd eaten what the ladies had cooked,
and the chores were all done to a tee,
We all gathered 'round the fireplace,
and sat 'round the Christmas Tree.
We sang a few carols of Christmas.
The little ones sang parts they knew.
Then Grandpa, he told 'em some stories,
of Christmas' past that he knew.
As the kids were almost asleep now,
dreams were stampeding their heads.
We carried them off to dream on their own

and tucked them all safe into bed.
We visited with the folks a bit,
arranged gifts beneath the tree.
We filled each stocking with loving care.
Then it's off to bed, for the folks, you, and me.
We'll dream of the things that we wanted to give.
Thank God, for the things that we've got.
But it's nice to be together at Christmas
and share love. In itself, that's a lot.

WRANGLING ON SMOKEY

We were bringing in the cattle off of the desert in July, headed to their summer range. As we got near the headquarters in Plush, we'd break camp and come in. We would wrangle the horses in the afternoon, catch the horses we would be riding the next day, and leave them in a lot behind the shop. That would save us having to run the whole cavvy to the corral in the mornings and save us a little time, sorting through the horses in the dark.

The lot where we turned our next day's mounts was the resting place of every old piece of machinery that the outfit had ever owned. It was about 300 yards long and about 100 yards wide. Right in the middle of the whole affair was a concrete loading dock that we used whenever we had to load machinery onto a truck. We would pull in a couple of wagon loads of loose hay and just let the horses eat it off of the wagons. To say the least, it was full of obstacles. The alkali dust would get worked up in this lot and be about six inches deep, as fine as powdered sugar. When this dust got stirred up, you couldn't see anything. We would usually pull down into this lot with a pickup after breakfast, honk a couple of times, and the horses would run right to the corral.

One morning I got up from the table at the cook-house and left while everyone was having one more cup of coffee. I grabbed my halter on the way by the tackroom, walked to the bottom end of the lot, and caught a gentle horse named Smokey. I jumped on him bareback and was just going to bring the rest of the horses to the corral. The horses were feeling extra frisky that morning and took off as hard as they could go, racing and bucking around that lot. Smokey joined right in the fun. At 4:00 in the morning, it's still about as dark as it is at midnight, and it was one of those nights that had no moon or star light. Pulling on Smokey, bareback and with just a halter, was like trying to stop a freight train.

All that I could think about was what it was that we were about to hit, and there wasn't any way that I was going to jump off at full speed, which seemed to be the only gear we had. On about the third trip around that lot, things suddenly got worse. In came the boys in the pickup to wrangle the horses.

By this time, the dust was stirred up enough to almost make you use the windshield wipers to see, and I wasn't near as worried about what we might hit anymore as much as I was worried about what might hit me if I fell off. About three or four more trips around the lot, and my noodle legs were quickly losing their endurance. The horses took one last trip to the bottom end of the lot and stopped in the corner for a split second. I bailed off, jerked my halter off of Smokey, dodged the pickup, and walked back up to the corral. By this time, everyone is busy catching their horses.

"Where have you been?" asked Con, the person who had just wrangled in the pickup.

"I was on one of those horses that you've been chasing around for the last ten minutes." I replied.

"See, Jerry, I told you that was a hat we saw go through the headlights that one time."

I've often wondered in the back of my mind, if somehow the corral gate didn't get shut for a few extra trips around that lot.

FREE VERSE

What is this stuff, they call free verse?
    It makes no sense to me.
It wanders like a plumb green colt,
    and has no rhyme-er-ry.
I has to have a dictionair,
    to look up half the words.
Like searchin' for a cowchip,
    once the meadow's dragged for turds.
Like a pen of singles cattle.
    There's every shape and size.
There's every breed and color.
    Then I starts to realize,
It's still a pen of cattle.
    Under hide, there is red beef.
But better them, to make the sorts,
    and save me all the grief.

BROWN'S QUITTIN'

Sometimes when a feller decides he's gonna quit an outfit, the best thing to do, is just quit. It seems that if you try to prolong it, it just turns into a case of hard feelings.

We were helpin' a neighbor brand one spring, and it seemed his hired man had been in a quitting mood for quite some time. Now Lee was a good hand and had worked on a lot of different outfits. When the boss told him that he was flankin' calves wrong, it was the straw that broke this camel's back.

"Look, you little whipper-snapper, I was flankin' calves before you were ever born. So don't you be tellin' me how to flank calves," says Brown. He then left the corral and started putting a gather on his belongings.

Nobody said much, until the boss said, "I suppose he's gonna quit."

"Well, that's the way I'm lookin' at it," I said, "but just being here for the day, I don't really know."

When we were done branding, Lee came over and asked a couple of us if we'd help him load some heavy tool boxes. We told him sure. He told us that he was quittin' that so and so. The boss' little kid was there and jumped up on the fence. With a real questioning look, he asked him, "What's wrong? Don't you like my dad? Don't you like him?"

"Sure I like him, son," was the reply. "But It takes ten thousand acres for him and ten thousand acres for me just to get along. And there's just not twenty thousand acres up here."

P.G.G. FEED STORE

Every little feed store and co-op is
the same, all across the country.
Some just have more than others.
As far as atmosphere and good
people, that's pretty constant. This
poem was written about Pendleton
Grain Growers, who had co-ops in
both Pendleton and Hermiston, OR.

I went into the P.G.G.,
    to get me sack of feed.
They had baby chicks and parakeets,
    Assorted garden seed.
They had them there pettunies,
    and roses, trees, and shrubs.
Insecticides and homicides
    for any types of grubs.
And tack for my ole pony,
    that would dress him fit to kill.
I even buyed a new hat,
    my old one's feelin' ill.
They had that fertilizer,
    by the sack or by the barrel.
One peek in that ole hamster cage,
    you knowed they wasn't sterile.
They even had them tropical fish.
    I seen ole Roger catch 'em.
He'd get his little dip net,
    and this is how he'd fetch 'em.
He'd swoop and swipe and holler,
    then he'd trap 'em 'gainst the glass.
He pinned one agin' the rim of his net,
    and that one lost his ass.
But ole Roger's got a fine soul,
    and he throwed him in for free.
He quickly gave "the sign of the cross",
    and said, "No extra fee."
And Coleman's in the back there,
    just a sellin' up the wire.
He's got nettin', barbed, and barbless,
    and that kind that lights your fire.
Poor Gay's been runnin' circles,
    'till he nearly has dropped dead.

I think it's high blood pressure.
    His hair's a turnin' red.
And Ellis, he's the boss there,
    and he runs a ship shape crew.
No matter what the order,
    they can get it there for you.
And it seems they're always pleasant.
    The nicest folks you'll ever meet.
If they don't have it, they can get it.
    And for us, that's pretty neat!

A NEW KIND OF CIRCLE

This poem came out of wintering out around the
Boardmen, OR, country on farm circles. We went
over to that country from North Powder, OR,
when I ran cows for the 7 Diamond.

A circle was something you did with the crew,
    and you did it on horses with legs.
But now I find, it's a field of corn,
    and a hot-wire put up on some pegs.

And campin' out. We used to do that.
    Lived in teepees to gather and brand.
But Holy oh Moses, it's five months of the year,
    that we're stuck in the corn and the sand.

But the weather's not bad. Or so they say.
    Not much snow, so not too much hay.
And we live in a trailer with a rug on the floor.
    Damned wind'd, blow a teepee away!

But they're right about snow. They haven't got much.
    But this fog and freezin' rain.
It takes a chisel to do the work of a broom,
    and the damned stuff is cold just the same.

But they don't last long, the winters here.
    Go to grass, three months before June.
And to calve in a place that ain't twenty below,
    makes a man whistle a might brighter tune.

STYLE WITHOUT OPTION

Ron, a friend of mine, tells me of a wreck that he was in:

I've got a bull roped one time, and I've had to take a few extra dallies, just to hold him. My old horse blows up, and goes to spinnin'. I'm tryin' to get clear of the wreck, but I'm havin' trouble gettin' those extra dallies off. By the time I do, that bull and horse are all wound up and tied pretty short. I don't know how it happened, but all of a sudden, I'm just standin' along side of things. About that time, the two of them go down and roll into the bottom of this ditch. They're on their backs, and all eight legs are kickin' holes in the sky. About that time, my mecate comes tight. It's somehow fowled in my belt, and I'm jerked right in on top of the pile. The feller that I'm ridin' with, shows up about that time, and says:

"I like your style, son. To think that you were completely free of a wreck like that, and you jumped right back in. Now that's spirit."

ODE TO TOAD

*Toad was a black horse that I rode when I worked
for Lynch Bros. in Plush, OR. He made as fine a
bridle horse as I have ever ridden, and his character
was one that fit me to a tee. We certainly had a lot of
fun together. I think that when I left the outfit, that
black horse was the hardest thing to leave behind.*

I had a friend, his eye way kind,
    his coat was black as coal.
And the white on his face and the white on his feet,
    he'd had since he was foaled.
We'd trotted across the desert,
    and gathered in aspens, gold,
And been up high, where no cow should be,
    after a heavy snow.
We'd been to lots of brandin's
    and worked a rodeer too.
We'd even gone to town at times,
    to see what we could do.
When we worked, we worked. When we played, we played.
    Some times it was hard to say,
Which was which, and what was what,
    but we enjoyed it either way.
Though circumstance has parted us,
    to his memory I will cling.
When and if I get to Heaven,
    I hope he's waitin' in my string.

IN-COMING

A rodeer is when a bunch of cattle are held without the aid of a fence or corral. They are bunched and surrounded by the cowboys, and then the sorting or branding is done. Sometimes it can happen in a fence corner, but they aren't actually inside of a pen. At times, it can be a terrible job, "holding rodeer."

If the weather is cold and nasty, a person can near freeze just sitting there for hours. If the weather is warm and the cattle are holding good, it can get boring and catch you or your horse half asleep when a cow tries to make a break.

This story was told to me by my brother-in-law, who was the indirect cause of the wreck. The direct cause was deer getting into the alfalfa stack. Now if these deer weren't tearing up the alfalfa stack, the Fish & Wildlife wouldn't have given them any shell crackers. These are noise making devices that you shoot out of a twelve gauge shotgun. They go whistling along and then they make a loud "pow". The fact that the neighboring outfit had a big rodeer going right alongside of the road was coincidental.

This outfit ran brangus cattle, and the boys had about two or three hundred first calf heifers in a bunch, working out cows that had lost calves and cattle that weren't going to calve 'till late. Now these cattle are holding good, and it's about the first time that it's been really warm all spring. The boys holding herd were getting bored. You could tell this by the way they were all sitting all humped up, resting their arms on their saddlehorns. One ole kid has his leg cocked up over his horn, and they're all messin' with their hats—a sure sign that they are all suffering from an excitement deficiency. Monte cranks in one of those shell crackers and lets it go, right out over the rodeer as they drive by.

It seemed to liven the cowboys right up, and even the cattle are cured. The boys were able to keep what they had worked out and the remainder of the herd from mixin', but just barely and not without considerable running about. They were a little short handed when things really got exciting, as a couple of these daydreamin' cowboys woke up a little later than the horses they were ridin'.

It's funny how what some people find great humor in, others find it hard to laugh about until quite a few years later.

PAYIN' YER DUES

*This poem is kind of a combination of
three different bronc rides. The first I
heard about, the second I saw, and the
third was a bronc called C. Clyde. I
guess all three riders were just payin'
their dues.*

*The one that I saw was one of the
prettiest bronc rides I ever saw Con
Lynch make. We seemed to take on a
few horses that people just wanted
some miles on when we came in off of
the desert. The reason most of these
horses weren't getting rode much was
that they had the buffalo on whoever
owned them. Although the setting in
the poem is on the desert, this
particular ride happened in the
graveled yard at the "27," Lynch's
headquarters.*

*Con had just untied this horse from the
hitchin' rack, got his snaffle on him
and stepped aboard, What happened
next is still a pretty picture in my mind.
A young cowboy on a showy buckin'
horse, makin' all the right moves to get
him covered. I'll never forget how he
kept coming up on one side of the
electric wire that went to the light on
the loading chute, then the other. This
old horse was getting some air and
Con was tapped and settin' good.*

*C. Clyde was a bronc in a rodeo string,
and a little due payin' for a good friend
of mine, Jerry O'Sullivan.*

At daylight, he's been up for hours,
makin' biscuits and cakes out of sours.
    The coffee is hot;
    it's in a black pot
on the table; there sure ain't no flowers.

The cowboss, he lets out a squall.
For to breakfast, he gives 'em a call.
    "Get up you bumbs,
    come fill up yer tums."
Then he leans his back up to the wall.

We roll out and look for a light.
It sure looks like the mid of the night.
    We flap down the vent
    on the ole teepee tent,
then head for the cook-tent, all right.

We wash in a dirty ole basin,
then go in and get us some rations.
    The coffee is strong.
    Not long until dawn.
Then we talk about what this day's got facin'.

The boss looks into the night,
like he's lookin' for some kind of light.
    It seems strange to me,
    'cuz I sure can't see,
but it's there, it's just out of sight.

Then we go down and catch us a snide,
'cuz this day is a rock-poundin' ride.
    We all start to grin
    on the bets we might win.
The new kid would ride ole "C Clyde."

He tightens up on his reins
and gets him a handful of mane.
    His elbow is tucked,
    and if he should buck,
he's gonna get on just the same.

He don't take much time gettin' on.
Silhouetted up there in the dawn.
    We can see in his eye,
    that he's sure full of try,
Out here, where there's rocks for a lawn.

The ole horse, he's startin' to buck.
I sure wish this ole kid some good luck.

'Cuz I am the man
that's sayin' he can,
if he does, I can make me a buck.

Well, he gets through the storm that is bad.
I'm grinnin', he's sure made me glad.
He's paid up his dues,
just like me and you.
To the boss man he says, "How's that, Dad?"

JAKE'S WRECK

Now I'm personally not a big dog fan. Although I have been around a few dogs that were worth their salt, the most of them made me ride more miles and fix more fence, than if they hadn't been around at all.

I think that there are two reasons that come to mind of why there are not better dogs. The first is, that nobody does any ground work with them. They just get them to where they will follow and away they go to work. It's like everybody teaching their colts to lead, rollin' 'em in a saddle, and going out to work pairs.

The second is, that there is no canner market for bad dogs. I haven't been on any outfit that was against getting rid of a plumb bad horse. But you'd be amazed at all the people that will keep a plumb bad dog. Some ole three legged mutt that only attacks a cow when you're tryin' to get her through the gate he thinks he ought to be guardin'. It takes a pretty special horse to get pensioned instead of canned. But if you are a dog, you've got it made on most outfits.

That starts off a story about a dog that should have been on the first canner truck leavin' the outfit. Now I'm not mentionin' names, but if you were around the local store a few years back, it wouldn't be long until ole Jake's name came up.

The feller that owned this fine dog, also owned a bunch of cows that dearly loved to fight dogs. One ole cow would beller war, and cows would leave their calves for two miles, to come and join in the fray.

It happened at a brandin' in the spring of the year. This feller had just bought a brand new pickup, and we were usin the tail-gate for a table like you do. Ole Jake's layin' under this new pickup, mindin' his manners pretty well, until this ole cow follows her calf to the fire. Now this ole cow has her head right on the ground, her tongue's out, and she's bellerin' warnings of what she'll do if anybody touches junior. Now most of these ole girls are pretty much bluff, but every once in a while, a feller might run into one that means business.

Well, this ole cow is hangin' right in there, and one of the ground crew is swattin' at her nose. Right away, Jake sees that he's needed. He comes boilin' out from under that new pickup to join in the ruckus.

This ole cow is especially fond of dog meat and sure takes to him. But Jake just bails back in under that pickup and reaches out and nips her on the nose. This doesn't improve ole bossy's disposition any, and she tries to move that pickup to get to the source of her aggravation. It seemed that every time Jake surfaced, it was in a new spot. By the time a fast talkin' dog can bark three times, the whole side of that pickup was caved in.

Jake's owner called him some pretty bad things. But Jake being a dog, forgave him, and was sittin' right in the passenger's seat come next morning.

TEARIN' HAIR AND HOLDIN' AIR

Now Dick was a hand, you understand,
    that had no fear inside.
He'd tell of wrecks, and you'd expect,
    somewhere he should have died.
But here is one, that's lots of fun,
    I'll share it here with you.
It was tearin' hair and holdin' air.
    We laughed when it was through.
Things were grim, this bull won't swim.
    Bank's fifty feet away.
We had him roped, and what we hoped,
    was to drag him 'cross that way.
The roper knew, when he swam that slough
    that he'd be short of twine.
But he'd hold him true while the rest of the crew
    whipped on that bull's behind.
Well, we beat and we thumped, on that ole bull's rump,
    But we weren't havin' much luck.
We twisted his tail, 'till it was frail,
    but the bull just sank down in the muck.
Though the roper tried, he'd slip and slide,
    and out on the end of his rope.
He could not pull that sulled-up bull.
    Things weren't goin' like we had hoped.
Then the ole bell rang, and Dick, he sang,
    "I know what we can do.
If that horse would hump, and that bull would jump,
    we'd get him in that slough.
I'll jump on board, on the bull, I'll ford.
    You guys lead ole Jim.
I'll spur his hair, 'till he jumps in the air.
    Then we'll drag him for a swim."
So with a handful of hide, he prepared for the ride.
    The bull's tail, he would use for a rudder.
He spurred him firm from stem to stern,
    and some cuss words he did mutter.
Well, the old bull jumped, and the ole horse humped,
    and the bull headed into the slough.
He took a high dive and lit flat on his side,
    and his nose was all that's in view.
Now Dick's still on board, and the ole rope horse poured,
    everything that he's got into pullin'.

But the far bank's too steep, and that bull's in there deep,
    and the bull still wants to be sullen.
Now Dick's head's below, and Lord, don't you know,
    there's nothing that we can do.
Try as we might, that bull's in there tight.
    Dick, it looks like it's curtains for you!
Short time's quickly tickin', when that off-leg starts kickin',
    and maybe that bull starts to roll.
Through all of the splashin' and all of the thrashin',
    the top of Dick's hat starts to show.
Then the bubbles arose, and now, there's Dick's nose.
    Like a whale, there's a big water-spout.
He sputtered for air and just got it there,
    when that bull laid back down for to pout.
Then once again, that off-leg does begin.
    The eternal seconds do start.
Dick's adrenaline's flowin', that bull gets to knowin,
    them spurs will soon pierce his heart.
So the ole bull gives in and continues his swim,
    across the deep part of the slough.
And when he set sail, Dick still had his tail.
    Followed him out like a real buckaroo.

GO AND JUST BUCKAROO

They say, with barbed wire,
    came the fall of the West.
I ain't denyin' it's true.
'Cuz there's few places left,
    in this once empty West,
you can go and just buckaroo.

But you follow a fence,
    and you'll find gate or hole,
and there you can wander on through.
But the days are gone,
    when you took horse and tack,
And could go and just buckaroo.

For the East runs this land,
    and they don't understand
about cows or our points of view.
They don't even care
    if they're playin' square,
Or care 'bout some lost buckaroo.

But throw the gate wide,
    'Cuz I'm still full of pride,
and I'll fight 'em till my life is through.
And out in the West,
    when they lay me to rest,
I'll go and just buckaroo.

MCKEE'S HORSES

I asked Deese McKee how he got out of the horse business. I'd heard that he ran over five hundred head at one time and loved to hear his stories. Sometimes you kind of had to prime these old timers for a story, and then they still might not even acknowledge that you'd said anything. He gathered his thoughts for a minute before he started.

"Well, I'll tell you. I had about two hundred and fifty mares and colts turned out on the Beatty Buttes for the winter. I summered them over on Hart Mountain, and for some reason, they had come back over to the Post Meadows on Hart and got snowed in. It was during the Depression, and I'd found a job. By the time I got word that the horses were in trouble, I couldn't get the time off to go take care of them. I needed that job worse than I needed those horses. Come spring, there were just a few old mares left.

"The others, I had down on the main ranch. A feller came through and offered to buy them. He talked me out of a good team and wagon, so that he'd have a way back. He was going to trail the horses from Plush to Crane, where he'd ship them on the rail road. He was supposed to pay me when he got back. That was the deal, and that was the last that I saw of him, my wagon, my team, my horses or my money. And that's how it happened."

HAPPY

I've spent my whole life livin',
dreamin' through my pony's ears.
Done a heap of separatin',
sortin' out the sweat and tears.

Been a first calf heifer's mid-wife
in a blizzard's howlin' wind.
Shared my wood stove with them babies
on a bad night, eight or ten.

I've swam that ragin' current
just to save some dyin' calf.
Some tangle-footed, tryin' colts
made me sit and pet and laugh.

The sun-ups and the sun-sets
makes you close to Charlie Russell:
Swirlin' blue, the burnin' hair smoke,
spring brandin's dust and hustle.

Them baby calves a fightin',
or a buckin' through spring flowers.
Settin' waterlogged and soakin',
watchin' rainbows 'tween them showers.

The hide that I've left smokin'
on some dally's never found.
There's a little more that's scattered
'round some "homesteads" on the ground.

But I gotta say I'm happy,
and here's the reason why.
My wife rides close beside me,
and she'll be there till I die.

MCKEE'S CHILDHOOD

Deese McKee, an old timer in this country, told me of how it was when he was just a little feller:

"There were only three cow outfits at the time in this area. The "MC" in Adel, the "7T" here in Plush, and the "P" ranch over in Frenchglen. They didn't have the country all cut up with fences in those days. Each outfit had it's main crew, but also had "reps" at each of the other ranches. A feller might be working at say, the "P" ranch, and only be around Frenchglen once or twice a year.

"These cowboys were sure a lot of fun for a kid about seven. The only problem was, they would all ride out every morning and leave me no one to bother except the blacksmith here at the "7T" headquarters.

"When he couldn't stand me bothering him any more, he used to put me in a gunny sack, pull it up around my neck, and tack me to the side of the blacksmith shop. When I'd get mad and start yelling at him to let me down, he'd stop what he was doing, come over, and poke my head inside of the gunny sack, then go back to what he was doing for another hour. It didn't take too many applications of this until I was pretty "coyote" around him.

"The only kids that I had to play with was when the Indians would show up for their winter camp. They used to camp between the headquarters and Hart Lake. Dad was always glad to see them and would usually give them a beef or two. They would build their hogans out of anything they could find. Sagebrush, juniper limbs, bones, hides, whatever they could get their hands on. The smoke would be so thick in them that the only way I could breathe, was to lay on the floor. The Indians would really rib me about not being strong enough to stand the smoke.

"When they would pull in for the winter, Dad would always go out to greet them and shake their hands. They would tell him that he was different than most white folks. 'Most white folks see us comin', and run like son-a-bitches.'"

HOW CAMP GOT RUNNING WATER

When I was fifteen, my parents leased an outfit in the
north end of the Goose Lake Valley. This was the 70
Ranch, owned by Don and Maxine Hotchkiss. They ran
the cows up in the forest north of the place in the
summer, and in the winter, we ran out on the desert
about half way between Burns and Lakeview. These
cows went to their desert country in November and ran
outside until January. We'd then gather them up and
bring them inside to the cow camp until the first part of
April. They then went back outside on a permit on Little
Juniper Mountain until June, when we'd gather them
back up and take them in to their summer country
north of Lakeview. Cow camp was always a fun place
to spend time. Every chance we got to get away from
school and go to camp, you can bet that's where you'd
find me. We had a little bunch of registered cows at the
main ranch in Lakeview that Mom and us kids would
take care of, but on weekends us kids would head for
the desert to see Dad. On Christmas or Spring break,
we'd sometimes take care of the cattle on the desert
and let Dad come in and see Mom. I will always
remember feeding with the team Rex and Flax. A
person sure falls in love with a good team of horses.
Rex was getting a little old, and Flax would do most of
the pullin'. I can remember coming down the road with
a load of hay from the haystack. This was an everyday
chore and on the way back, the wagon would be about
ready to overtake old Rex. He'd be joggin' along lettin'
Flax pull the weight with his tug chains pretty slack. I
used to reach down and grab a few hairs in his tail.
He'd jump right up where he was supposed to be and
those tugs would be even for about ten steps, then he'd
start backin' off again. It wouldn't be but twenty yards
and I'd grab his tail again. It seemed to spook him just
as bad the last time you did it as it did the first, and
you could do it twenty times in a mile. When things got
tough though, and the pull was a hard one, Rex was
into that collar and givin' his all.

The cow camp at the desert was just a little trailer, a
set of corrals, and two big lots. We were only "inside"
with those cows for about three months while they
calved. The water for camp was a well about 300

*yards from the trailer. We packed water in milk cans,
and Mom was always trying to get us to put in a
pipeline from the well, and put in a frost free spicket at
the end of it so she had better access to water. Beings
though we were always busy calving at this time, it
was a job that got put off until one day when we knew
it was time.*

A winter's camp, at Alkali Lake,
out under Rehart Rim.
And for a life of luxury,
well, it was cut down pretty thin.

No runnin' water in this camp.
We packed water from a well.
It's a story on my mother,
that I'm fixin' for to tell.

Now Mom would help with the daily work,
and Mom was a lot of fun.
No matter what the weather,
Mom was there 'till we were done.

She'd listen to all our stories,
take our abuse, and hear our lies,
But the day she milked out that big titted cow,
we saw fire in Mother's eyes.

Now she seemed real tame, for a range cow,
as we drove her to the lot.
Or maybe, her bag was just too big
for her to run or trot.

We jerked our ropes and stretched her out.
Left Mom there on the ground,
To relieve a little pressure,
on this beast that we had found.

Now Mother took right to her,
and she'd milk her down a bit.
'Till she figured that bag was down enough,
the calf could handle it.

And every time she'd squirt a stream,
it would puddle and would swirl.

Mom's face would wince with agony.
She was feelin' for the poor ole girl.

'Cuz that bag was chapped and sunburnt,
cracked and split, and awful tight.
Mother figured, when we turned her up,
she'd likely want to fight.

Now the cow had just been layin' still.
Had hardly twitched an ear.
From up where we were sittin',
it seems unfounded fear.

Now Mother's built like Santa.
Well, maybe not that tall.
But, she has his other features,
His rosy cheeks and all.

And Mother made us promise,
to let her get away.
She kept thinkin' that cow was "on the fight."
Mother's get that way.

But as soon as she had turned to go,
we pitched the cow the slack.
And instantly upon her feet,
she started her attack.

Now Mom was slowly climbin'
that corral of lodge-pole pine.
When all at once, a thousand pounds
of hate breathed down her spine.

That sort of shifted Mother's gears
and really made her rocket.
That cow was gettin' awful close
and snuffin' in her pocket.

Well, she nearly, almost, made it
when her diggers both gave way.
And it left her 'cross that upper pole
in a horizontal sway.

Her hands tore up the air in front.
Her hinders, kicked up the aft.

And if you would have been there,
you couldn't of helped but laughed.

That ole cow was jumpin' higher
than any one I'd seen at all.
With front legs, like them pogo sticks,
they sell down at the mall.

Then the ole cow finally reached her
and gave her feet a boost.
Not enough to really hurt my mom,
Just knocked her from her roost.

But, just as luck would have it,
tumble-weeds had grown tall.
And gathered on the outside there,
to break my mother's fall.

Well, the blue smoke billowed skyward,
as she stomped off to the trailer.
She never ever said a word,
but her eyes were talkin' "sailor."

And all the rest of that morning,
when we'd get from that trailer's view,
We'd get plumb down a laughin',
the way you sometimes do.

But you could have heard a pin drop,
when we sifted in to lunch.
And not a single word was spoken.
A pretty somber bunch.

And there upon the table,
unopened, in a dish,
was exactly what we got for lunch—
One can of "tumor fish."

But by night, Mom had softened.
Her kind heart could not repel.
And we spent ever extra minute,
diggin' pipeline from that well.

SUNRISE ON THE OUTHOUSE

This poem was the direct result of another poem, "How Camp Got Running Water." In that poem, my mother was the main character. My father really liked it because it was on Mom, and he just happened to be on the other end of the ole cow when we turned her up. Mom came to me and said, "To keep peace in the family, you better write a poem on your father." I asked her what I should write about. She told me not to tell him that she told me, "But he's scared to death that you're going to write a poem about the time he passed out on the outhouse."

Ma and Pa went out a dancin'
    before us kids was born.
And the story that I'm tellin',
    will still make my Father scorn.
It was just a small town gatherin'.
    The band weren't all that big.
But, Ma and Pa had drifted down,
    to dance themselves a jig.
And every time the band would quit
    or when their feet got sore,
They sorta shifted out in back,
    and the whiskey shore did pour.
Now Pa had taken several snorts,
    and Mother'd had a few,
and it seemed before they knew it,
    the dancin' was all through.
They sorta wobbled back to camp,
    shortly before dawn.
Somehow the ole truck made it,
    so they just parked it on the lawn.
Now Mother headed straight inside
    and headed for the sack.
But Pa, he thought he'd better check out
    that little house outback.
Now Mother, she went straight to bed,

and she was fast asleep.
Poor Father sorta passed out,
    as he sat there in a heap.
But in a couple hours,
    when the sun shone in his eyes,
he got a rude awakening,
    and it was a surprise!
For his legs had fallen dead asleep,
    as he sat in there and snored.
It seems his butt had swollen up,
    beneath that outhouse board.
He sounded like a champagne cork,
    Like he was vacuum sealed.
And his legs, they would not hold him,
    as he wobbled and he reeled.
He was hobbled as he wobbled,
    and he knew there was no chance,
of him a standin' upright,
    and a pullin' up his pants.
Well, he did the ole "watusi,"
    but he couldn't find his pins,
and it didn't take two seconds
    'till he was down again.
He finally got his pants up
    and crawled off to their abode.
You couldn't repeat a single word
    'tween there and that commode.
He really gave it to poor Ma.
    "Don't you love me? Don't you care?
I could have maybe froze to death.
    Or been eaten by some bear."
But she knew she had one on him,
    and I think he knew it too.
It's just another "spice of life,"
    that's been added to the stew.

THE TRADE-IN

The boss had owned this pickup for just about a year when this happened. He was coming in off of the desert from a trip around our permit there. He'd been lookin' at the feed and the water holes. He's late for something, and he's flyin' right along. Phil's been in a hurry all day long. The road that he was on at the time wasn't all that great, but the ones that he'd been on all day were worse than terrible. All of a sudden, he hits a big jump in the road, and his pickup quits. The first thing that he tries, is to restart it. Nothing. He looks in his mirror, and sees his engine laying in the road behind him. After a long wait, he catches a ride and makes it on into the ranch.

After a couple of days, he gets a mechanic, and they go back out to the desert to retrieve it. They get the engine loaded and tow the pickup on in. When they take a look, they see where the motor mounts have broke off, and the frame has spread enough to let the engine fall on through. They put a chain and binder under it and pull the frame together enough to get it to town to get things welded back together.

Phil is talking to the man that owns the welding shop, when the owner of the new and used car lot drives up. The boss and him are pretty good friends, and he is always trying to sell Phil a new pickup.

"What you need today, is a brand new pickup." Farley pipes up, not knowing any of the troubles.

"Now why would I need a new pickup? You just sold me this one last year." Phil replied.

"Well, I'm really in a tradin' mood today. If you'd trade that one in on a new one, I could give you a really terrific deal on one of the brand spankin' new ones that we just got in."

Phil smiles. "Well, I'm kind of afoot right now for a while, so let's go have a look at them."

After Phil looks the pickups over, he asks, "Well, what kind of a deal are you gonna stick me with this time?"

Farley starts the trade. "Beings though you're such a good friend and all, if you'd trade in the one that is down at the welding shop, I could let you drive out of here in one of these, for let's say, two thousand."

"That's a deal?" the boss asks. "I'll have to think about it."

After quite a bit of horse tradin', Phil has him down to fifteen hundred.

"I'm takin' a terrible loss here." Farley says. "But you do a lot of business here, and I'll do it."

"Do you want me to bring it up here?" the boss asks.

"No, you just go down and switch the stuff out of your pickup and I'll have the boys get it later. Then come back up and we'll have lunch," offers the car salesman.

"Give me ten minutes." Phil tells him and hurries off to the welding shop, before they go to work on his ex-pickup.

That night, he gets a call from his friend at the car lot. "You realize, don't you, that I really took it in the shorts on that pickup that you traded in today?"

"What do you mean?" says Phil, "That was a brand new chain and binder that I threw in."

WHEN HE RAN THE PLACE

This poem was written for Phil Lynch, a man that I had a great deal of respect and admiration for. I worked for the Lynches for eleven years and ran the cowboy crew for eight of those years. I'll never forget the first time I was really in charge of things.

I was twenty one, and although I'd been working there for three years, I wasn't really sure if I could handle the job or not. Phil assured me that he'd back me 100% and that if we made a mistake that we'd make it together. We always moved camp to the desert on July fifth. On the sixth, we trotted out to start gathering cows.

"Scatter your crew where ever you want them," he said. I was the oldest on the crew by four years, and I think that the youngest was twelve or thirteen. I sent two little kids trotting off this way, two more were headed off for a water hole, and so on till we were all headed out. Phil told me to come with him over to this knoll nearby. When we got on top, he asked, "Do you see anything wrong?"

I immediately looked behind me to see if I'd rode by a bunch of cows or something. Not seeing any, I replied, "No, I don't see anything wrong."

"Well, me either. I'll see you in November. I'm going to have my back operated on, and they are going to fuse a couple of discs." With that he rode off towards camp. All of a sudden, I was cook, baby sitter, and dishwasher. Callin' all the shots to get the work done and had to keep all of us kids alive doing it. Phil pulled up out there a ways and turned around and looked back. I was on the outside circle and needed to be in a long trot. I waved goodbye and saw him in November.

When I first knew him, he ran the place.
An upright man with finesse and grace.
A man who had a dream in life.
A dream he could share with his kids and his wife.
He'd change the things that "Pops" wouldn't do.
The things changing times will make a man do.
He'd raise his family with strength and pride,

And hope for respect till the day that he died.
He'd run the place in a business way.
He'd run the place and make it pay.
In the palm of his hand, he had it all.
Just stay on top and right on the ball.
But change things did, when ole "Pops" passed on.
Somehow this much tax wasn't counted upon.
Was it a few cows bought that didn't work out?
Or too many days of the flood and the drought?
Did "Uncle Sam" play too big a hand?
Or was it the changing times across this land?
Or might it be, he had it too good,
and just got lazy and didn't do what he should?
Was it a life of hard knocks that took it's toll?
Or too many days in the heat and the cold?
From aching bones turned old too fast?
Or things Mother Nature just wouldn't let last?
What ever it was, he gave up hope,
And each new day was a slip of the rope.
He turned to the bottle, to help out a bit,
and it soon overpowered him, and in it he fit.
For his family and life, oh the price that he paid.
And soon as it does, there was no other way.
By the time he'd believe, there was only one out.
He died in a bed when we pulled the plug out.
I'll miss this old man, though young was his age.
For in my life's book, he filled more than one page.
I'll always remember the good with the bad.
He could make it so good, or he could make you so mad.
But deep in my heart, lies a place where he stays.
And I'll always remember, when he ran the place.

THE SCARED PICKUP

The Irishmen in this country have quite a sense of humor. No matter how bad the situation seems at the time, they can always look back and find something humorous about it. Their way of describing events and mishaps is sometimes even pleasant to the ear.

An Irish rancher and his hired man were headed to the high country early one spring, to check out a couple of cows that they had heard had wintered out. It happened to be on a refuge permit. Now sometimes the roads were open, and sometimes they were closed, depending on the particular frame of mind that the refuge was having at the time.

This particular day the roads were closed with a white, single pipe gate. It was simply a three inch pipe that hinged on a post on one side of the road and was chained to a post on the other side of the road.

It was a bright sunny day, and the sun shining off the packed, crusted snow, made seeing difficult. It was a simple oversight, as they sped on through the gate. By the time it was noticed, their windshield had been shattered and was laying in their laps.

The rancher admitted that the kid that was traveling with him was fairly tough though. By the time they found the cows and drove the sixty miles back home, it was dark and quite cold. Henry was describing his day.

"There we were, driving through snow country, on a bright sunny day, when we drove through this gate. To think that they painted it the same color as the snow. Well, we hit it a pretty good clip and it shattered our windshield. It scared me. And it scared Con. And it scared the pickup."

REE'S TABLE

I made a table out of old barn wood
for my mother-in-law, Marie Price. I
put this poem in the drawer.

I know this drawer looks empty,
    but it's only how it seems.
'Cuz it's stuffed plumb full of memories
    and promises and dreams.

And every time you open it,
    a new one can be found.
If it's not the one you wanted,
    simply sit and dig around.

'Cuz in it – is every baby calf
    you've watched on wobbly knees.
And every good ole bridle horse,
    you've spun around with ease.

And every dog you've ever known,
    the puppies and the cats–
the places and the settings–
    every ridge and draw and flat.

All the people that you've rode with,
    movin' cows or brandin' calves–
The thumps, the bumps, the wisdom knots–
    the bandages and salves.

There's deer and elk and coyotes–
    Sun and rain – and wind and snow.
Hot dusty times in summer–
    Icy temperatures below.

But mostly it's a gift of love,
    from all of us that can't be near.
That's why it's filled with memories.
    And hope and love and cheer.

So now you know – this drawer's not empty.
    It's only what you see.
'Cuz there's a gift from everbody,
    that has ever called you Ree.

ONE HUNDRED MILES AN HOUR

My brother-in-law and his family went to a barbecue over in Frenchglen one time and came home with this story.

It seems at this barbecue there was kind of a smart aleck kid that no one really cared for. When I say kid, I mean in his late teen or early twenties. He kept hangin' around some of the cowboys bothering them, until Gary finally told him in no uncertain terms to just get lost and not be around him any more.

It wasn't long until Gary found out that all of the beans hadn't been cooked upside down and had to go to one of the two little porta-potties that were there for the barbecue. This kid that had been pesterin' everybody, saw his chance to get even at Gary for callin' him down, and slipped up behind the one that Gary was in, and pushed it over on the door. His next mistake, was when he rolled it over, so Gary could get out.

For those of you that don't understand porta-potties, they're little plastic out-houses. The only difference between them and a regular out-house, is that a regular out-house sits over a hole in the ground, and a porta-potty's hole has a floor in it, so the raw sewage can be hauled back to the plant. When they are tipped over, there is nothing to keep what's in the basement from coming right on up to the main level. When Gary came out that door, he was hobbled, dipped, and on the fight.

Gary didn't even bother to pull his pants up before he had a fist in that fellers face. Gary knocked him down, then dove right on top of him and pounded a little of what was on him, out of that kid. Gary finally took a little breather and got up and pulled his pants up. As he did, he got his first good look at himself. He was covered from head to toe. It wouldn't be good if it was all your own, let alone a mixture of a couple hundred people's. He got him a handful and went to work on that kids face with it. No one stepped in to help that kid, for two apparent reasons. One, he certainly had it comin'. And two, no one really wanted to touch either one of them.

When it was all over, the door on the other porta-potty flew open and out came my niece Lacey. She must have been

68

about seven or so at the time. There was just a little blur that made a bee-line to her mom. "I couldn't tell what was going on out there Mom, but I heard a lot of words that I'd never heard before, so I finally made a run for it and ran one hundred miles an hour straight to you."

RED RIVER CORRAL'S PACKER

When we left the Seven Diamond in
North Powder, OR, we went up to the Elk
City, ID country and worked for Billie's
uncle who had an outfitter's business at
Red River. We packed mules for him that
summer and fall. We went back the next
spring and guided a bear hunt and got
all his mules shod up. I hadn't spent
any time around mules before and
hadn't packed much before, either. We
had a great time and got a whole mantie
full of poem material.

Ladies and gentlemen,
  horses, and mules.
Wilderness trodders,
  and hard huntin' fools.

You come to ole Red River,
  for to hunt and fish and play.
Some of you live in Idaho.
  Some come from far away.

Some come for summer pack trips,
  a vacation in the hills.
Some of you come to see the sights,
  or have some fishin' thrills.

Some come to leave it all behind.
  They come out here to play.
Far from all their pressures.
  They come to "get away".

When huntin' season rolls around,
  and them hunters come a runnin',
everything that does need done,
  will surely keep you runnin'.

You pack 'em in and pack 'em out,
  and take 'em what they need.
You never ever grumble,
  'bout the things that they won't need.

You simply catch another mule.
    If you run out, pack the dog.
I've seen some of them fellers,
    owned the whole Cabela's catalog.

Some of 'em want a trophy,
    they have their sights set high.
Some of 'em find, to bag an elk,
    it takes a lot of try.

I've got an elk to pack at Finnigan.
    They need more whiskey at Burnt Knob.
When I get home, I'll shoe a muie.
    It's all part of the job.

Some of 'em want a drop camp.
    Pack 'em in and let 'em be.
Some of 'em want a guide and cook.
    It's all the same to me.

'Cuz I'm the lonely packer,
    The tender of the stock.
The one who gets no credit.
    But, who works around the clock.

HALF AN INCH OF THAW

He's up, he's down,—He's up, he's down,
he sits there on his chin,
while the cow is headed somewheres for the herd.
Then he makes a mighty gather,
and he finds himself again.
What I thought too loud, the girls all thought they heard.
Then he quickly gets his speed up,
and he goes to shut it down.
The whoa is but accelerated coast.
And though he beat the cow there,
and she didn't get away,
somewheres in the stop, you split a post.
But you have to give him credit,
for he does the best he can.
He's not cold-jawed, or is he plumb outlaw.
He's just a workin' cowhorse,
givin' everything he's got,
in frozen lot, with half an inch of thaw.

FIDDLES

There's something almost mystical,
    in them magic fiddle tunes.
Like swans, a flyin' over head,
    and callin' to the moon.
Like a bull elk, calls his challenge,
    or a coyote, changes keys.
There's something in them fiddles boys,
    that makes you tap your knees.
Well, they picked the Harp, for Heaven's Door
    But folks, let me tell you what.
I hope in Western Heaven,
    they got them fiddles, sawin' hot.

PEG LEG

I heard a story one time of a man trying to load a horse in a small truck. It seems this colt didn't want to lead in, so the man had tied his lass rope onto the lead rope, ran it through the side of the rack up towards the cab, and was now behind this colt with the tail end of his rope giving him some added incentive. The colt jumped in just as this couple rounded the corner of the road and were passing by where this colt was being loaded. As the colt jumped in, the feller loading him ran around the side of the truck to tie him in. Unbeknownst to the couple in the car, this feller had an artificial leg. About the time that he reached up for the lead rope, this colt decided to unload again and came flying out backwards. The poor feller happened to get a coil of rope around his false leg and was jerked up the side of the truck. At least until it jerked that fake leg off, leaving a boot and one leg tangled in the rack of the truck. He quickly gets up, hops around to the rear of the truck, and catches his colt before he takes off. The couple that just happened to be going by at the time, ran off the road, and totaled their car.

HATS

I wonder, if your ole hat could talk,
    what stories might unfold?
You know, the ones that it has seen,
    but you have never told.

Of all the places in it's life,
    that it has come to rest.
I wonder, if your ole hat could talk,
    what story'd be its best?

Like the time when you fell off your horse,
    fell flat off and hit the ground.
And you were glad no one else was there,
    'cuz you'd never live it down.

Or the things that you have told someone,
    when they were miles away.
But when you got right next to them,
    you couldn't find them words to say.

Or the tales of the opposite gender,
    that might have took a run at you?
What if that ole hat could tell us,
    what you did—or didn't do.

Of all the absent minded things,
    that only it has known.
And all your silly day-dreams,
    and the settings they have shown.

Of your miscalculations,
    that were so important at the time.
And all your dumb inventions,
    that were never worth a dime.

Why, your ole hat is with you,
    more than your ole horse or Rover.
But if you're like me, you'd just soon be
    gone, when they talk things over.

MORE ON HATS

I was just a wee bit of a lad,
of maybe seven years.
And the story that I'm tellin',
to my eyes, will still bring tears.
I was out to help my papa.
Probably mostly in the way.
And things weren't going smoothly.
Dad was having a "bad day."
We had taken the little truck,
and stuffed it full of cows.
But when we backed up to the chute,
it didn't fit somehow.
Too big the cows, too small the truck,
the load had too much weight.
The chute is sittin' four inches high,
and we've got a damned drop-plate.
So now we've got to jack her up,
and block up both hind tires.
Give our load a little boost.
Make her sit a little higher.
I was searchin' 'round for blocks,
and Dad would run the jack.
Then something really tickled me,
and I couldn't hold it back.
Now father thought upon his hat,
there fell a little mud.
But what I saw was mighty green,
and from the wrong end of the cud.
The brim of father's hat filled,
'till the structure did give way.
Then it withered and folded downward,
in a most distasteful way.
Well, father wiped his eyes,
and saw me laughin' there at him.
And I knew by facial expression,
that my good time just turned grim.
So I lit out a runnin',
just as fast as I could go.
And father was in hot pursuit.
What's on his mind, I didn't know.
But I did know that it wasn't good,
for me to stand around.
So I squirted through the corral poles.

Dad had to climb, or go around.
My size was my advantage,
and I was able to get away.
My father quickly cooled off.
But I still hid for the rest of the day.

SILVER SEA OF SAGE

*I've taken several people that are from
some big city, out into the high desert
country. The remarks are nearly always
the same. The silence is deafening. The
vastness and lack of people is frightening
to them. They realize their insignificance to
the world as a whole. Mother Nature has
once again put them in their place.*

Like a shining shrine, the sun comes up,
    o'er that silver sea of sage.
The rays enhance the newness of the dawn.
    The vastness of the land rolls out.
A never ending game.
    A game in which man plays a simple pawn.

PORTA POTTIES

I've heard a couple of other stories about how dangerous these little porta potties can be to travel in. One story came from down in the produce growin' country in California and was related to me by a friend of mine named Joe. Joe had a porta potty business at the time and would supply porta potties to all of the fields that were being hand harvested. He usually had two houses on a trailer and would just pull into a field and unhook the trailer. That way he didn't have to spend all his time loading and unloading houses.

It was getting late in the evening, and they needed to move a trailer. The field where the trailer was at, was finished, and the trailer's destination was about three hundred miles down the country. They were in a hurry, so they just hooked up and went.

When they got to where they were going, after bouncing over several rather rough railroad tracks, out steps a rather irate little Mexican gal from one of the houses, much to their surprise. It didn't really surprise them that she was mad, just that she was in there.

It wasn't very long before she had a very nice motel room to clean up in, brand new clothes, and a very nice rig and driver to escort her back to her home.

NO CLOWN IN THE BARREL

On another occasion, I heard of a bull that bailed out of the arena at a rodeo and went out through the crowd. It seemed that this old bull was sure on the fight and takin' whatever got in his way. Before the cowboys got a rope on him, he mistook the porta potty for the clown's barrel and gave it a pretty good toss through the air. It came apart as it hit the ground, and what was in it, was all over the ground. Including a lady who happened to be using it at the time.

You just can't be safe anywhere these days.

LONG RIDE IN THE WAGON

Another porta potty story was told to me by Lee Earl, a friend of mine from Asotin, WA.

Every year, they put on a trail ride from Asotin, WA, that concludes in Joseph, OR. It's rodeo time when they get to Joseph, and they really whoop it up in the parade. There is usually over a hundred people mounted.

On one of these rides, they were all mounted up and had hit the trail for their next camp. After the riders were fed breakfast and had left, the support team would break camp and move it on to where they would be spending the next night. They failed to notice the extra horse tied up over in a thicket of trees.

When the potty trailer stopped at their next campsite, out pops a cowboy from one of the porta potties. There he was, afoot, with his horse tied up some twenty miles back.

A feller just can't be too careful around those things.

MONGO

*This is also a true story. It was told to
me by Mike Donaldson who was the
buyer. Jimmy Alves, the brand inspector
in those days, said that the owner was
a little embarrassed, so I'll let you figure
out if it's your neighbor or
someone else's.*

It's early in November,
    and the calves are set to go.
And something rarely seen by man—
    The trucks—not one "no show."
The steers are weighin' deep in "five."
    The heifers, slightly lighter.
And the price I got was out of sight.
    Things ain't looked much brighter.
The bunch is pre-conditioned, weaned,
    none bawlin' for their mother.
And damned if they aren't uniform.
    They look like one another.
But standin' out amongst 'em,
    is one that's just not right.
His ears, well, they been froze off,
    and his hide don't fit him tight.
His hair is dead. One eye is blue.
    His jaw's a little lumpy.
You know the kind.....Hard luck life.
    He looks a little dumpy.
Leppy. Bummer. Doogie. Dwarf.
    Whatever he might be.
Everybody knows one.
    The kind you hate to see.
He lives on what the others leave.
    He robs the best he can.
He'd get pushed away from a feed-bunk
    if he was alone there in the pen.
But you hope he'll go unnoticed.
    You hope to slip him by.
'Cuz you'd surely like to get rid of him,
    'cuz the booger just won't die.
He's cost you more in shots and pills,
    than he'd return if you sold him twice.

And though you treat him regular,
  he just won't shed them lice.
But at last they're weighed and ready to load,
  and the buyer, he's all bubbles.
And though he hasn't said a word,
  you feel you still have troubles.
Then he took on a fit of laughin',
  'till I thought that he might choke.
"That four year old, you threw in there,
  he's really quite a joke!"
My face turns red. I try to smile.
  Tears are so hard to keep in.
"You mean, MONGO don't get to go?
  This year, ...Again!"

PERCY'S PAIR

Percy's pair came in the ring,
    and they're about to die.
The cow's got nearly forty irons,
    and there's tired in her eye.

Hip bones like spread buzzard wings
    and draggin' one hind pin.
She's no stranger to this place.
    It's sale day—again.

And her calf? He ain't much better.
    With his tail all flat and matted.
Muffled laughter can be heard
    amongst the farmers as they chatted.

Then up the ramp a packin' coffee,
    miss "busty" Russel, don't you know.
And if you'd ever seen her,
    well, you'd seen a large eye full.

I thought we'd all die laughin',
    when the auctioneer did start 'em.
Now there's a healthy pair, boys.
    Not one bad blemish on 'em.

KA BOOM

It is said that Plush once was home for around 2000 people when the mining was at its peak, the sheep were around, and the hotels were running. It now is the home for maybe 45 people and consists of a general store and saloon with a gas pump. What a change. I bet things were pretty lively back in them days.

I heard a story about the proprietor of the old White Hotel having trouble keeping fire wood. It seems the boys would come in of an evening, have a drink or two, maybe more, then as they left, help themselves to an armload of dry wood on their way off of the porch. He figured he had devised a plan to catch the guilty parties. He stacked his wood until it was above eye level, then set muskrat traps all along the top edge of the pile. Then all that he would have to do is look for black and blue fingernails and peeled up knuckles. This was quite effective for a short time, then the wood began disappearing again. The crafty critter was not falling for the trap.

The proprietor took more drastic measures. He took a chunk of firewood, cut the end of it off, drilled a hole down the center, filled that with black powder, and nailed the end back on. It seems that one of the local ranchers ended up with the loaded limb. His newly wed wife had a batch of biscuits in the wood stove and decided that one more piece of wood was needed to get them that golden brown color.

In a very short time, the biscuits and stove lids were scattered about the kitchen. Then all that the proprietor had to do was find out who was ordering a new stove. I heard that nothing was ever said, but the wood outside the White Hotel was never touched again.

FOR HART MOUNTAIN

*Plush lies at the bottom of Hart Mountain. It
is the home of Hart Mountain National
Antelope Refuge. I wrote this poem the year
before they kicked the cows off. About the
only thing that hasn't come true is that they
have not paved the road.*

Let's make Her all the way She was,
    before the White man came.
Let's save Her and protect Her,
    'fore She knows more White Man's shame.
Let's fence around Her boundaries.
    "Hell, She's not going anywhere."
Let's take away all signs of man.
    Tax monies, show we care.
Let's pave the roads across Her,
    so that thousands, come to see.
The mighty things we've done for Her,
    this land, that we've kept free.
Let's take the cows, from Her good grass,
    'till it's decadent, coarse, and dead.
And Her wildlife has gone, where cows still graze,
    where there's tender plants, instead.
Let's overpopulate the coyote,
    'till there's no new fawns to live.
Let's save Her and protect Her,
    'till She has no more to give.
And when She's a mat of weeds and brush,
    that's choked itself to death.
Let's have a "TOTAL CONTROLLED BURN,"
    and snuff out Her last breath.

THE BLIND HEIFER ATTACK

We were busy gathering the desert, heading for our summer range. We'd been camped out about ten days and were planning to run in that night for a shower and something besides my cooking. We had the cows as far as we were going to take them that day and had gathered a cow that was blind in both eyes. She had a baby calf, and we didn't think that they'd make it in all the way and still be together. I told the boys we'd just put them on the trailer and take her to Plush. I'd trot our horses back to camp, then just bring my own pickup in. We planned to put her down by the lake where she'd have easy pickings and wouldn't have to travel for feed or water.

When I got the horses taken care of and into the ranch, I asked the boys if they had doctored that cows eyes before they turned her out. No such luck. Beings though all of our horses were on the desert, that kind of left us in a pickle. We figured we could just rope her out of the back of the pickup. She was just a first-calf heifer, and not too big or strong yet.

The only ropes we could find were some thirty footers out of one kids rope bag. These two kids I'm working with are both good hands, and I didn't think that it would be too tough a job. I'm driving, and they're standing on the back bumper. I'm simply going to drive by this ol' girl, and they are going to step off and rope her. Sounded good.

This ole heifer is sure wild and isn't going to let that pickup anywhere near her. No trouble. I just apply a little more pressure on the gas peddle. The heifer couldn't see, but she could sure hear good and was bad to duck off.

Jerry finally jumps off and gets her caught. He's in a foot race and used about twenty eight feet of his rope just getting' to her. It fits around her neck though, but he doesn't have enough left to get sat down and hold her. She escapes.

The heifer is dragging' his rope and headed straight for this big flood ditch. It's dry, but I figure she'll break her neck when she falls in as fast as she's going. I pull up along side and honk the horn. The horn must have been out in the lead by a nose because she turned ninety degrees into me, and hit me with her head right in front of the driver side door. This spins her around, and she uses her whole body to cave in everything from the door back. She comes off the end of the pickup and falls into the ditch anyway. I knew that she'd loose her feet when she hit the bottom, and I bailed out and was sitting on her before she could get up. I didn't get too much help from Con and Jerry. They're busy rolling around in the grass, laughing, and holding their bellies.

"How bad's my pickup?" I asked. This question cost me another five minutes of laugh time before I could get any help.

Like I said, there's not much mercy on these outfits.

ACRES OR ACHERS

"How many acres do you have?"
the pilgrim asked of me.
"I have a right good many,
though there's some that you can't see.
There's some that's buried deep inside,
and though you can't define 'em,
there's others on the surface,
if you look, well, you can find 'em."

This sort of caused a questioned look
upon the pilgrim's eyes.
I could see by his soft and lily hands,
he didn't realize,
that acres, has two meanin's,
no matter how they're spelt.
There's acres, used for measurin' ground.
And there's achers, that is felt.

Like the time that bronc unloaded you,
when your rope strap finally broke.
Then he kept a comin' up your back,
a breakin' every spoke.
Or when you were workin' cattle,
in the chute with worn claw,
and it come a bustin' open,
and a breakin' up your jaw.
Of all the little wisdom knots,
that swelled with polished pride.
Or the ones that's buried deep inside,
like when Shep or Baldy died.

So, you ask how many achers?
I got a pair I'd give to you.
We simply could trade places.
Instead of me, this could be you.

You were runnin' hard to turn a cow,
and hit a bog, forlorn.
Your horse did stop with instant speed,
as you drug 'em cross the saddle horn.

89

EAGAN'S WRECK

Now most of the old timers in this area were of Irish decent. My father leased an outfit from one of these ole characters one time, and the neighbor said, "Bye, and yer the first White Man to move into the valley for over a hundred years."

Most of these old timers were born in Ireland and had never driven anything but a team of horses. When they came here, they were introduced to the car. I have heard lots of stories about their notorious driving, but this one has just come to mind.

The local store was closed on Thursdays, so the owner could go to town and restock his supplies. Now if the store was closed, and Mr. Egan couldn't go there for a beer, he simply drove the extra forty miles on into Lakeview. On one such day, Mr. Lynch was headed into Lakeview when he sees Mr. Egan on his return trip home. Now Mr. Lynch was aware that Mr. Egan was not the best of drivers, so he pulls off into the barrow-pit and waits for Mr. Egan to pass by. On nearing Mr. Lynch, Mr. Egan begins swerving and ends up hitting Mr. Lynch's parked pickup, head on.

"Oh, Mr. Lynch, I'm so sorry. It was all my fault," said Egan.

"No, Mr. Egan, it was not your fault. It was my own," said Lynch.

"How do you mean, man. You were completely off the road and parked, and still I hit you. It was my fault, and you go into Collin's Motors there in Lakeview and get yourself a brand new pickup and charge it to me," offered Egan.

"No, Mr. Egan, it was my fault. I have known that on days that the store is closed you go to Lakeview. You've been doing it for years. I had no business on the road."

GO SEE

With all that is not known,
    lies a certain mystery.
The kind you can't be sure of.
    The kind that you can't see.
Some things you take for granted,
    but it's only in your mind.
So go and get it first-hand.
    It's the only way to find
what's right and true and honest,
    or what is false and lies.
What's found might be just one man's guess,
    without any truthful ties.
We take too much for granted,
    "Someone" told us it was so.
The only way to be sure,
    is go and learn and know.
Don't be afraid to doubt someone,
    'til you know that he is right.
Don't be afraid to say you're wrong,
    when you've found his credit's tight.
Don't be afraid to explore the plot
    of something told for fact.
And if you find the facts are wrong,
    don't be afraid to act.

THE MESSAGE

A lot of times a cowboy will change country for the winter months. A feller by the name of Twain Stockdale was working for me one Fall when I was up around North Powder, OR. It was getting pretty wintery out, and we were out gathering one of the last truckloads of cows to ship down to the corn circles around Boardman, OR, then we'd move camp down there. We'd just split up when Twain pulled up and asked me, "Did you hear that?" I didn't hear anything except blowin' snow. Every time we'd get together that morning he'd ask me if I heard that. Finally he told me that he heard it good that time and it was callin' "California, California."

Twain moved down to Boardman with us. Him and a green kid were livin' in one little trailer and Billie and I were in another. One night he came to me and said that he'd got a letter from the California reined cow horse association. "I got it a couple days ago, but figured it was just dues so I didn't even open it then. Come to find out, the mare I've been showing this summer has earned enough points to be eligible for this big show. I think I'm gonna pull the pin on you and go get her ready," he told me.

"Just a minute before you get all excited and quit," I told him. "Maybe you ought to kind of weight things out here." He kind of looked at me puzzled and asked what I meant. "Well, let's look at what you've got here. You're hand loadin' and feedin' 150 pound bales of weedy alfalfa hay and got hay fever so bad you can't hardly breathe. You're living in a tin box with a kid that's askin' you about 2000 questions an hour. And don't forget all this fine freezin' rain. Now what do you have in California? A girlfriend. A good bridle horse. Warm weather. What are you still standin' here talkin' to me for?"

"I was hopin' you'd understand," he said smiling. We shook hands, and he headed out hard for California.

It's a message sent from far away,
that only some can hear
that comes a callin' on a certain day.
It might be ridin' on the wind,
or on a leaf that falls,
that starts a great migration on its way.

It can trumpet from a new-born sprig,
that's finally broke the ground.
Echo off a steamy hillside in the spring.
Who knows just where it's hidin',
or when it makes it's call.
'Cuz most of us no longer hear the thing.

But the Caribou, all hear it
as do Salmon, Whale, and Dove.
The Capistrono Swallow hears the ding –
The Buzzard and the Meadowlark.
The Goose, the Duck, the Swan.
Before the fence, the Bison heard the thing.

But most of us don't hear it.
Though we did in early times
when being nomads was the normal way of life.
Instead of stuck in cities,
or to jobs we can't forsake,
we "pulled the pin" to save our life some strife.

But in any kind of culture,
or in any form of life,
comes a "throw back." Seems to happen, now
and then.
The "breeding" outs in eye of cat,
or color of the hair,
to remind us of our past and where we've been.

When it gets down below zero,
and the fog has set right in,
It seems to have a cold all of its own.
And though everbody shivers,
'cuz it chills you to the bone,
it causes driftin' cowboys for to roam.

I think that every cowboy hears it,
though he doesn't always go.

He might winter where the Artic winds do howl.
But he dreams of runnin' cattle
where they don't pitch any hay.
In a place where winter's weather's not so fowl.

They don't chop ice. They don't pitch hay.
They don't wear rubber boots.
They don't chip frozen calves up off the ground.
They don't wear fifteen layers,
and their ears are never froze.
Excuse me, but I thought I heard a sound.

A single strand of horse hair,
ain't the size of garden hose.
From the frost that's been a buildin' over night.
And when works all done, no packin' wood,
no waitin' on the warm.
The bunkhouse, it stays toasty all the night.

Their horses, they're all shed off
and feelin' strong from grass.
The calves are all turned out and on the gain.
Their feet don't break, as they step off,
their fingers never numb.
Excuse me, but their goes that sound again.

The sound is kind of muffled.
It seems buried in this drift
that I'm diggin' out to get the gate to swing.
But with every single shovelful,
it keeps a gettin' stronger,
'till once again, I clearly hear the thing.

So I think that I'll just follow it,
'cuz it's a headin' South.
Not nothing goin' here, but feed till spring.
And I'll see just where it takes me,
and what lies in it's path.
'cuz I was born to listen to the thing.

94

NOW GO ROLL YOUR BED

On a lot of the big outfits, they used to use nothing but single men on their cowboy crew. This was more when they had camps and "pulled a wagon." These were sure different times than they seem to be today. There was always a big turnover in the crew, and the cowboss didn't much know about a new man until he had been around him a while.

Now just because a cowboy liked to move around a little and change jobs, didn't mean that he wasn't a good hand. A lot of these fellers just liked to see new country and ride new horses. Kind of see how different outfits worked and meet new people. Some were running from something, but most were just changing country. Nothing was considered wrong with this, and if a man was a good hand and got along, he was help if he worked a month or a year. If you told the boss that you were "rolling your bed', it meant that you were quitting. If the boss told you to 'roll your bed', it meant that you were fired. A good hand was always welcome back, if work was available.

On the other hand, a lot of men couldn't hold a job for one reason or another and were always 'rolling their bed'. Maybe they were poor help, couldn't get along with the bosses or the crew, or had a fight going with a bottle. This is a story that I heard concerning the cowboss at the "MC", and a new kid who had just hired on.

They had just mounted and already the cowboss had his doubts. By the way this kid had handled his horse getting him caught, and saddled, Hugh had his suspicions that maybe he didn't know as much as he had let on. As they started out, the new kid's horse blew up and started bucking.

He immediately dropped the reins, grabbed the saddlehorn with both hands, and went to screamin'. The ole horse quit bucking and just sold out running. Hugh was running after them, yelling at him to pick up his reins, and stop the horse. After a couple of miles, he got close enough to reach down and pick up the reins, and stop the kid's horse.

He just sat there, glaring at the kid and said, "Why didn't you pick him up like I told you?"

"I was too scared," the kid said trembling.

"Scared of what?" Hugh demanded.

"Scared of fallin' off," the kid replied.

"Well, is everything better now?" Hugh asked.

"Yea, I guess so," the kid said, as he relaxed his death grip on the saddlehorn.

"Good," the boss said, and immediately pushed him out of his saddle. "Now go roll your bed."

CIRCLE

Thank you for the little things,
    you give to us each day.
The newness of each rising sun,
    the meadows full of hay.
A spring that's full of baby calves,
    a wife that's close beside you.
A spring that's full of wild flowers,
    each petal kissed with morning's dew.
A summer's sun and long hot days
    when a man can reach his peak.
A horse that trots beneath you,
    and never does feel weak.
A fall that's full of sortin'
    and taking home of stays.
The crimson shades of autumn
    the peaceful autumn's haze.
A winter when land takes its rest
    and lies beneath the snow.
Though cold and harsh, it seems to say
    in spring again I'll grow.

BUCKOFFS IN GENERAL

Now getting bucked off, is generally funny. But usually only if you are the one who didn't just take the big crunch. The people who weren't just in the wreck usually have a comment or two about what you could have done, what you looked like, or how you landed. Usually the first question asked is, "Are you all right?" If there is a reply, and you aren't hurt too bad, they'll either start right in on you, or if a person is overly cranky, give you a little time to cool off. But you can bet that you are going to hear about it before the day is over. These are a few comments that I've heard:

"Look at all this air, and you can't find any of it."

"Your flying's pretty good, but your landing's sure need some work."

"You landed just like a fifty pound sack of taters."

"Why did you get off?"

"I think you might land better if you'd keep your head higher than your feet."

"I thought we'd need a crane to get you out of the hole you made."

"Getting a license to fly?"

"Why did you turn him loose?"

"Good thing you landed on your head. You could have gotten hurt."

"Taking up a homestead, I see."

"Lots of achers out here, isn't there?"

"I've told you and told you that all you have to do, is keep your mind in the middle and a leg on each side."

"Good thing that rock was there to break your fall."

"I think you might have got him covered, but when you went to quirting him, he got mad."

"Kind of drove your ol' butt up around your ears, didn't it?"

"You're getting to where you can get off of either side of that ol' colt pretty good."

I've also heard some pretty good comments from the ones who have just eaten the dirt. I heard about a kid getting bucked off in a meadow one time, and it seemed that he slid face down on a fresh cow pie for quite a ways. When the boys asked him if he was all right, he rolled over and said, "I'm not really sure. I see green."

I heard about another feller that got bucked off on his feet one time. He's just standing out in front of his horse, still holding the bridle reins. He turns to the boys and calmly asks, "Did any of you see what I did with my gloves?"

Now buckaroos, have always been known for their fancy silver buckles and conchos. A feller will get several thousand dollars tied up in a fancy rig, and still put it on a fifty dollar snide bronc. I heard about a kid that got bucked off pretty hard one time and tried to point at his horse, who by this time had quit bucking and sold out running for God knows where. His shoulder was broke, so he raises his other arm, points, and says, "Save the silver."

AT LAST IT'S SPRING

Can you hear it on that reckless wind?
Can you smell it, as it thaws?
Can you touch it, as the frost goes out?
When the wind, puts up it's claws?
Can you taste it in a morning sigh?
Can you hear that blue bird sing?
Can you feel the new, in your very heart?
At last , I think it's spring.

John Lane and Dick Otley at a branding. Photo by Cindy Lane.

Author roping calves at spring branding. Photo by Cindy Lane.

Branding fire. Photo by Cindy Lane.

Author adjusting propane branding pot. Photo by Cindy Lane.

Old time 7T crew: left to right, Ed Suterland, Chas Cleland, Frank Chico, Leon Frakes, Deese McKee.
Photo courtesy of Sylvia Cleland.

Chas Cleland driving horse buck rake, bringing loose hay to the stack, late 1930s.
Photo courtesy of Sylvia Cleland.

Stacking loose hay. 1939.
Photo courtesy of Sylvia Cleland.

300 P Ranch mules. About 1913.
Photo courtesy of Sylvia Cleland.

THE WHITE WOOLIES

All cows can get cranky if you get them mad and corner them to where the only place they have to go is over the top of you. Some cows are just born mean. A cow that's been a little shy on groceries or water can get a bad disposition in a hurry. Add a few thousand lice and a little pain and maybe that old cow will just remember you from a previous experience. I'm not really sure which category the cow I'm about to tell you of falls in, but she was pretty thin and full of lice.

Now, Roy didn't like to ride much, and he was out about eight head of cows. He had finally got them spotted in a field that lay next to one where we were wintering. As I remember it, it was pretty froze up. Beings though we were down there a- horseback quite a bit, he asked if we might get them for him some day. We told him sure, as we did a lot of trading work back and forth back then. Something that has all but disappeared on these ranches anymore, except for a branding every once in a while.

We take off one morning with nothing more on our minds than to get that neighbor's cows. We'd had some moisture before it turned cold and snowed, and the only way you could tell if the alkali flat you were crossing was covered with ice and snow or just snow was to cross it. If your horse did an extreme amount of slipping, it had ice on it too.

Like I said, it was pretty froze up and cold, and Dick, the feller that I'm riding with, is wearing a pair of white woolies. For those of you that don't savvy "woolies," they're angora chaps. These chaps are made from the hides of angora goats, and they leave the hair on them. They come in a variety of colors, and are sure good at keeping a little of the cold off your legs.

Now, Roy's cows have a reputation to uphold on being wild and liking to run. I've stopped wild horses with more respect for a man a-horseback than these old cows had. When we finally get to them, it's apparent that they aren't going to let their reputation slide an inch. The race was on. You could get to the lead of these ole cows, but you couldn't slow down but one. The rest would just scatter and come around you. Sort of like they all planned to "meet-up" somewheres up the country, and there wasn't any rules on how to get there.

After the first splitting and scattering, I'm short one cow and my partner. A couple of more miles on up the country, and I notice these old cows aren't showing any more respect, but they are starting to run some slower. I finally get them to take down about thirty yards of fence, so they can be on the right side of things, and drift on home after they've had their little meet-up. I headed back, looking for my partner.

I finally came to a place that looked like someone has dragged a full grown cow through two or three inches of snow. From here, the trail is easy to follow. When I finally get to where the tracks end, things aren't happy. The cow is down and is complaining about being used for a trailer.

My partner agrees that we are through the drift fence, but it has turned into a matter of principal that the old cow is delivered all the way home.

When things get down to a "matter of principal," it's awkward for an outsider to come in on such a situation. There are options. You can say that it's hopeless, foolish, and a waste of time, and ride off. This you will never be forgiven for. No matter how hopeless and foolish.

The second is to jump right in and help – even if it means "better a dead one than a dumb one."

Third, you can go along, until one or the other gives in or has a flicker of common sense. Just the fact that someone shows up, sometimes will sway a stand-off one direction or the other. This is by far the best option to start out with.

After a little persuasion on the ol' cow, and a few comments about her condition, the owner shows up in his pickup and says to let her go. "She'll come on in by herself now."

This lets me off of the hook, on the one that Dick is going to be mad at. It was kind of a no-win situation.

In about a week, the mad has wore off, and we are down at Roy's, helping him vaccinate his cows and delice them. The cold hasn't let up any, and Dick is still decked out in his white woolies. As we get to the back side of the field and start to make our gather, the first cow Dick hits is this same old dier. The mad is back in full swing.

She's burrowed into a big patch of tules and has no intention of coming out for any reason. The first act of belligerence by this old girl and down comes Dick's rope. Before he can even get his slack jerked, the cow goes down. Now we're right back where we left off last week. Except that any love between them has simply evaporated.

"Get off and get that ole cow up," he tells me.

"Hell, it isn't any use. The best thing we can do for her is to bring her out something for her lice when we're done with the others." I replied. No consolation.

"I'll show you how to get a cow up," he says angrily and steps off with his quirt. After a severe thumping, he realizes that the cow is just too weak and takes his rope off.

"One more kick in the nose just to show you who's the boss," he said. The ol' cow gets up and takes to him.

For those of you that have never been around tules, after the wind has tipped them over, it's like trying to run on a suspended net. The worst of it was, the ol' cow catches him not expecting it, and he tries to run backwards. About two steps, and his spurs tangle in the tules, and he goes down on his back.

This ol' cow is too weak to hurt him, but she'd sure like to. She's blowing snot all over him and bellering war. All I can see are two white hairy legs, kicking at this ol' cows face. Laughing, I ride in and get the cow's attention. She takes a couple of steps towards me, and Dick gets up and tries to run again.

This old cow can't think of anything more filling than the cowboy that's been dealing her so much misery and doesn't stay at all interested in me, once Dick moves. After two or three times of that ol' cow dining on him, he gets away.

"Why didn't you rope her?" he asks all bent out of shape.

"I would have, but she wasn't hurting you any, and besides, it wasn't my fight."

TWO NEW ANGELS

This poem is dedicated to two little girls, Jenny Cleland and Katie Schadler, who fell through the ice and drowned. It was a sad day in the Warner Valley.

Two new angels were born today,
    as hand in hand they travel away.
To a place in which unfolds and flowers.
    For HE has called with HIS omnipotent powers.

And only in faith, can we see HIS way,
    as hand in hand, they travel away.

To a place in which HE groomed with care.
    For all of HIS children, to come and share,
the peace and love, that comes their way,
    as hand in hand, they travel away.

And many a rock has shed a tear,
    for those in our hearts, we held so dear.

Until upon some given day,
    with HIS guiding hand to show the way.
Just like those two angels, that were born today.
    Hand in hand, we'll travel away.

HORSE TALK

Have you ever wondered what those horses might say,
as they're ran to the catch corral, day after day,
and the cowboys step up for the next in their string?
I've often times pondered on this sort of thing.
For there's good and there's bad in both horses and man.
There's them that can't do it, and them that sure can.
There's them that don't want to, and them full of try.
You can usually tell both by the look in their eye.
So I listened one morning as they finished their oats,
and these are a few of their very own quotes.

"Now Ed, he's a good one. I'd like in his string.
He's got enough sense to teach you some things.
He's gentle and quiet and has a light hand.
He teaches and does things you'll soon understand.
At something new, he'll give you some room.
He don't expect it all before noon."

"Yeh, just backwards and sideways to that twister called Jake.
He'll beat ya and thump ya. And his spurs'll rake
your tired ole hide till it's bloody and sore.
And he'll yank on your face till he's got your mouth tore.
He's got a bad temper. He flies off at the bat.
And it seems that his horses soon turn out like that."

"Then there's Fats – he's so slow, he can hardly get on.
He moves like molasses on a cold winter dawn.
He always starts out just two jumps too late.
And he's always behind when you get to a gate.
It seems to me that it'd sure help somehow
if that lazy old buzzard, could out-think a cow."

"Now Bill, he's a corker. All laughter and smiles.
He's fun to be with as you log in the miles.
He works his cows right and treats us plumb fair.
Gets along with the crew and don't seem to care,
if the weather is sunny or cold or it's wet.
He'll be there each morning. A pretty safe bet."

"And the new kid, he's honest. But he surely is green.
But he listens and watches. And to me, well, it seems,
with some time and some miles, he'll be one of the best.
So I'll teach him what I can. Let time do the rest."

"Well, it sure makes a difference how they treat us somehow.
But I'd still rather be here, than pullin' a plow."

I WON'T NEED ANY FOOT-ROPE

Now on most outfits, a man was responsible for keeping his own string of horses shod up. Someone might offer to shoe one if you were hurt or behind, but it wasn't something that you asked another person on the crew to do unless you had a pretty good reason. If you did ask for help, you usually shod a horse for him or traded the favor in some other way down the road.

Now the boss was having trouble finding the time to get his horses shod one busy spring. Instead of asking any of the crew to do it, he hired a man out of town that had put up his shingle as a horse shoer.

When he showed up, I told him that one was a new horse the outfit had just bought at a sale, and the other was a colt, and it would be his first set of shoes. I told him that I didn't know first-hand about the new palomino gelding that we had just bought, but that I had heard by the grapevine that he was nasty to shoe behind. I offered him a foot-rope if he didn't have one with him.

He told me that he wouldn't need a foot-rope. I told him that the paint gelding was gentle, but he might need one on him, beings though it was his first time. Again he assured me that he wouldn't need a foot-rope.

I had other things to do, or I thought that I might hang around and learn a few tricks. When I got back, I found the yellow gelding with two front shoes on, but not finished, and the other gelding with no shoes, and this note:

"I don't shoe outlaws. The yellow horse is bad, but the filly needs lots of work."

He was right. He didn't need a foot-rope at all.

MY BEDROLL

This ole bedroll's my companion,
    though I've cussed it when it's damp.
I sure am glad to see it
    on a cold night back in camp.

Sometimes it's been my suitcase
    for to store my extra wares.
I sleep the best with stars above,
    where I don't have a care.

I can't say it's always comfort,
    for I've laid it in the rocks
on a place that isn't level.
    It's seen its fair share of knocks.

But, if I should die tomorrow,
    no casket, velvet lined.
Just lay me in my bedroll,
    and I know that I'll be fine.

LYNCH LOSES THE HORSES

A couple of old time Irishmen, Con Lynch and Teddy Baker, were coming in off of the desert. They were pulling their horses in a little open topped, two horse trailer, and they had a pretty good hill to come down. It was terribly wash-boardy, and about half way down, there was a switch-back. As they took the first corner, they lost their trailer. As they came around the next, the trailer, with their two horses balancing the tongue, came shooting in front of them and straight on down the hill.

"Bye!" said Con. "We have a trailer and a couple of horses that look just like that."

WISDOM KNOTS

*Anything that doesn't cripple permanently is
known as a wisdom knot. These can also be
mental bruises. Someone once said: "A failure is
not a failure if there was a lesson learned."
That's a wisdom knot.*

I'm tucked down in my blankets,
and I'm burrowed deep tonight,
  for the storm that's been a brewin' has arrived.
But my belly's full of warm food,
and my teepee keeps me dry.
  Men caught on nights like this, without, have died.

And I get to thinkin' backwards
to the places that we've seen.
  My bedroll and my teepee are old friends.
We've stood our ground together
through heat and cold and snow
  Just takin' on what Mother Nature sends.

We were camped out on the desert.
It was on her maiden voyage,
  and that was over twenty years ago.
Just a brandin' up the slick ones,
ridin' colts and havin' fun.
  We were salty little punchers, brass and bold.

But it seems the reckless freedom
of our youth is quickly spent.
  Lookin' back, it makes you wonder how one lives.
Through all the wrecks and tumbles,
those — the wisdom knots you've tied —
  and the learning by the hard knocks that it gives.

And a feller seems to slow some
when he's hurt some past repair,
  and the quickness of his youth is in decline.
You look for easy places.
You look for ways around
  the jolts that in your youth you thought were fine.

But the memory of them lingers,
and your thoughts are still alive,

117

and sometimes you can feel just how it felt.
When some old bronco's head went down,
and you with loaded spurs,
    drove 'em in the neckline of his pelt.

Every grunt and squeal he made.
His feet a tearin' sod.
    The way the leather is your saddle sings.
There's nothin' short of dyin'
that sets a soul alive,
    like a good ride on a buckin' bronco brings.

But those trips — they are all done now,
for you haven't got the speed
    it takes to get just half a ride half rode.
More eager for the gentle ones.
More wise and understanding.
    Learnings from the wisdom knots you've stowed.

Yes, I'm burrowed in my blankets,
and I'm tucked in deep tonight.
    For the storm that has been brewin' has arrived.
But as I lay here dreamin',
I wouldn't change a thing.
    The youth, at least in mind, has been revived.

JOHN'S BUCKIN' HORSE RIDE

There was a green kid working with us one summer, as we gathered off the desert and headed for our summer range. He was sure having hell with his horses and spent a little time walking while we chased loose horses.

One day we were eating lunch while we waited for the cattle to "mother-up" a little. All at once, a bunch of calves headed back for where we'd just come from, looking for their mothers. We all jumped on our horses and headed off the wreck. This kid had fallen asleep in the shade of a sagebrush and was a little bit behind gettin' on. He jumped up and got on his horse, and right away, this ole horse goes to taking big ole high jumps with him.

"Stay with him kid, you're makin' one hell of a ride."

"Ride that pot licker."

As the ole horse finally just gave up and stopped, the kid swelled up bigger'n a toad and hollered, "I finally got one covered."

We all rode over and shook his hand and congratulated him. We told him how good he looked and how hard the horse had bucked. Sometimes a little back-slapping and encouragement can sure build a green kid's confidence.

As we rode off, the ole horse didn't want to untrack and kind of humped up. This kid knows he can ride him now and is ready for whatever the horse throws at him. One of the crew looks back an offers, "Maybe you ought to get off and unhobble him."

CLOSE

Bedded deep in the ground
in that rodeo dirt,
lay a boy with no air
wearin' just half a shirt.
His lights were half off.
His world's spinnin' round.
He'd been real content
to just lay on the ground.
But somewhere real close
was a ton of pure hate,
and there on the top,
was his name on his slate.
That bull was a hunter
that ate human hide.
Men that don't move,
were the ones that had died.
So he tried hard to run,
but forgot to stand up.
He crawled on all fours,
like a three legged pup.
He finally did
get his legs under him.
He ran like the wind,
knew his chances were slim.
He looked like a waffle
when he hit wire mesh.
He tried hard to climb it,
regardless of flesh.
Height was his safety.
Get up or get through.
He knew in his mind
what that bull planned to do.
Three gallant attempts
before it was cleared.
My God, he was safe now.
Oh, how that crowd cheered.
A huge sigh of relief.
He looked back again,
to an empty arena,
and a bull in it's pen.

A MILLION KINDS OF COWBOYS

There's a million kinds of cowboys,
 and these are just a few.
From the farmer in his "bibbers,"
 to the wild-ragged buckaroo.
There's them that pack two ropes apiece,
 in the gun racks of their Ford.
There's them that pack one rope for years,
 'cuz it's all they can afford.
There's them that work for wages,
 and them that own the place.
Some of 'ems big and burly,
 some wear calico and lace.
I've seen 'em wear their spurs all day,
 and never see a saddle.
I've seen 'em in their hats and chaps,
 and never get astraddle.
I've seen 'em ride into the night,
 hours before dawn.
The same get home some after dark,
 and they've trotted all day long.
I've seen 'em on their cycles
 with wheels, two or three or four.
I've yet to see a uni-cycle;
 that'd be going just too far.
There's them that couldn't rope a lick,
 and them that's made of twine.
There's them that think that broncs be canned,
 and there's them that think they're fine.
There's yippers, yappers, yodelers,
 and them that whip and spur.
There's them that hardly say a word,
 but they're cowboys, just as sure.
There's them that work their cattle,
 and them that cattle work.
There's them that call 'em all by name,
 and seem to make it work.
There's them that run in thousands,
 with a small, well mounted crew.
There's them, it takes a hundred men
 to brand up just a few.
There's them that run 'em in a chute.
 Won't hardly let 'em stand.
There's cows that see men twice a year

for shippin' and to brand.
There's them that's surely forked
    and can ride like they were glue.
For some, to weather a good fast trot
    is all that they can do.
There's them that drink good whiskey.
    There's them that roll their smokes.
There's them with different attitudes,
    that wouldn't touch a coke.
There's wanna-bes, I'll tell you,
    that darn sure look the part.
It seems for them, the way they look
    is by far the biggest part.
I've seen slouch hats and gumbo boots
    make a bridle-horse sit and slide.
I've seen 'em in the best attire
    that couldn't even ride.
So cowboys, pick your poison.
    Run a bunch or just a few.
When you think you have the perfect way —
    just ask someone does it different than you.

LITTLE TOWNS IN EASTERN OR.

Now Paisley has its "Skeeter Fest,"
and Wallowa has its lake.
There's lots of little bitty towns
on the east side of this state.

Diamond has its craters,
Meachem has the Blues,
Minam has a little grade,
and Union's paid its dues.

Alfalfa grows a little hay.
Burns can get real hot.
Hereford has a white-faced cow.
Granite has one block.

There's a Brothers and a Sisters.
You can find an Antelope.
Did I mention Echo — Echo.
Iminaha has a slope.

But one thing they have in common,
it's the folks that call them home.
They've found a just excuse to stay.
That's why they never Rome.

DIXON'S TRIP TO SCHOOL

Now just South of where I live, is an Indian reservation at Fort Bidwell, CA. Years ago, a lot of these Indian kids would drift off the reservation and get jobs in the hay fields for the summer. In the fall, a wagon would come through and gather up all of the kids that needed to go back to school again. There weren't too many of these kids that thought too much of going back, and if they resisted, it was just policy to tie them up until they got back to the reservation.

They pulled into a ranch one fall, and asked Cecil, this older feller that I used to work with, if there were any kids there that were needing to go back. This is how he related the story to me:

"We were just kids at the time, I suppose fifteen or so. My brother, Clevon, was down in the field raking hay with a team of horses. He was rather dark complected, and he had quite a tan. I figured that with some luck, they might mistake him for an Indian. I told them that he would probably swear up and down that his father was the boss of this here outfit, but that they shouldn't believe anything like that. I told them that he was sure enough an Indian, and it wouldn't hurt him a bit to further his education. I also mentioned that he was quite a scrapper, and they'd probably have to tie him in the wagon.

"Off they went, and I was sure right about him fightin'. They had to take him by force, but they finally got him tied up and in the wagon. He put up a pretty good fight, for his size.

"About a week later, he broke out and came home. The only thing that he must have taken any classes in, was boxin' because he sure gave me a good thumpin' when he found out. I doubt if he finds a whole lot of humor in it yet today."

FOR LEA

*This poem is dedicated to Lea Flynn Harlan who died
of cancer. Always a special friend.*

Lea, oh Lea. At last your pain's set free.
You filled our hearts while here on earth,
    with loving memory.
And though we can not see you now, you always will be near.
For what you gave, amongst us, was love and grace
    and cheer.
You've been an inspiration to anyone you've ever met.
To say that you were Heaven sent would be an honest bet.
And now "His Calling" is complete. You've gone a better way.
We'll hold to the strength you've given us and
    meet another day.

    I've just been sitting here between heifer checks thinking
of the great experience that Lea must be having now. The
many friends and loved ones that she must be meeting. Tom
Jones, her uncle Phil, her grandparents. The ancestors that
she never got a chance to meet before. And all of the "new
country" that she gets a chance to fly. But most of all, to
stand before God and know she has nothing to hide. She'll
make a great Angel, just being Lea. It lightens my heart.

CON GETS KICKED OFF THE JJ

It seems that if a person looks at a problem from all directions, the answer is sometimes simple. This is a story told to me by Phil Lynch, about an experience that his father Con had.

I had just pulled into the yard one morning in the fall of the year, when my father pulled in behind me completely tickled about something.

"What's up, Pops?" I asked. "What's so funny?"

"Why I've just been run off of my own property," he told me.

Right away I got in the fight and asked him what he meant by that.

"Well, I saw a vehicle driving up into the upper end of the JJ this morning. So I thought I might go up and see what it was about," he told me. It was during deer hunting season, and Pops didn't allow any hunting in there and always had trouble keeping people out.

"When I asked these hunters what they were up to, they told me that they had permission from the owner and strict orders to run off anyone that they found on the property. I told them that I was sorry and that I'd get right out of their road."

"Well, I'm going to go right up there and run those people completely off the place," I told him.

"No lad, look at the problem. We always have trouble keeping people out of there, and these people aren't going to hurt the deer population any. If they can run me off, I'm sure that they will keep a pretty good eye out for anyone else."

SWEET AND SOUR BIGHORN STEW

*In the fall, I guide hunters. Bighorn
Rams get you into some of the most
difficult and beautiful country that
there is anywhere around. They are
hard work, but a most remarkable
animal. They have a more rigid
pecking order than a cavvy of cranky
saddle horses and are a great
pleasure to watch.*

This stew starts in an envelope
    the mail man has brought.
It says that you have drawn the tag
    that every hunter's sought.

So you hurry down and buy that tag
    before they change their mind.
'Cuz you know this stew is special.
    It's so sweet, one of a kind.

Then your mail box gets flooded
    from every "stuffer" livin'.
And every guidin' outfit,
    takes their turn at "B.S." givin'.

So you pick the help you're wantin'.
    It's best to keep it few.
Then four months anticipatin',
    the taste of this here stew.

And as the time draws nearer,
    it seems you're growin' weak.
'Cuz the pressure of a stew like this,
    doesn't leave much time for sleep.

But the hunt starts in the morning.
    (What's one more night without a rest?)
And early in the morning,
    you'll give that ram a test.

But it's hours in the glasses,
    till your eyes are burnin' red.

No chance for constant wind out here;
    it seems to swirl instead.

But still the call for Bighorn Stew –
    it echoes in the cliffs.
On every boulder, rock, and slide,
    on every wind, it drifts.

So I'll give you my best recipe.
    We'll start it up tonight.
The only thing we're missin'
    is the part that makes it right.

You take two quarts of water,
    and you pour it in a pot.
Keep the temperature real even –
    not to cold, but not too hot.

Take them guide and "stuffers" letters
    and rip them up petite.
Stir it in real slow now,
    'cuz that helps it taste real neat.

Take that torn up cartilage
    that bites in your right knee,
and add a couple gallons sweat,
    and hide and blood and — gee,

finely chop whatever's left
    from the soles of either boot.
Then dice a smelly sock or two,
    and add that to the loot.

The scabs that's still a bleedin',
    from that fall there in the rocks.
And all the little scars and dings,
    that's new on your gun stock.

Add all the air that's missin',
    'cuz you just thought that you were fit.
The blisters, and the owies.
    Even ones you won't admit.

Then take the sights you're gonna see,
    and in a separate bowl –

it's best to rinse your spoon off here,
    and stir these up real slow.

One step away from eagles,
    as they circle down below.
The rock wrens are so gentle,
    that they land right by your toe.

The lichen, ancient as it is,
    that has a million shades.
That grows on even older rocks.
    The one's that God has made.

The feeling that your gonna have,
    in awe of good sheep country.
That maybe man isn't as important,
    as we think we ought to be.

The grandeur of the canyons,
    the cliffs, the rocks, the slides.
Everything you get to see,
    as you search for white back-sides.

The spots you thought impassable,
    but oh! you made it fine.
The smell of sage and brush and bush,
    fresh air that is sublime.

Then take a good crisp morning,
    with frost or heavy dew,
let sunshine slowly warm it,
    then add it to the stew.

Then slowly mix these separate bowls,
    and simmer them forever.
And as you're reminiscing,
    Enjoy the hunt we had together.

THE PINK SLIP

It seems like every big outfit always had a good bucking horse or two on it. These horses might not be in anybody's string but were always handy in case someone got to braggin' a little too much. It seems the way our insurance laws are these days, a lot of fun and learning has been taken away from these young cowboys. This isn't a story about bucking horses, but more about chicken insurance laws.

This cowboy hires on to this big outfit in the middle of the winter. He seems to savvy an ole cow and his horses all right, and on the first day, they are working some cattle out of a rodeer. For those of you who don't know, there is a big difference between a rodeer and a rodeo. A rodeer is where you hold and work a bunch of cattle without the aid of a corral or lot. Sometimes there might be a fence corner or a fence along one side, but sometimes there isn't a fence around for miles.

Like I said, it's in the middle of the winter, and they are workin' cattle out of a rodeer. This new hand jumps his horse out to head off a cow, slips on the ice, and goes down. Not the cowboy's fault or the horse's. Just slick ground and no one is hurt. The next morning at breakfast, there's a pink piece of paper in his plate.

"What's this?" he asks the manager.

"That's a pink slip. A safety infraction," the manager tells him.

"Well, what does it mean?" the new kid inquires.

"Every time that I hear of something that could have been serious, even if it wasn't, I issue those involved a safety infraction. I heard that your horse fell down with you yesterday. If you get three pink slips, it's policy that we let you go. The same goes for the horse, if he falls or bucks three times, we sell him."

"Well, it wasn't my fault or the horse's," the kid explains.

"It doesn't matter," the boss replies.

"Well I guess you better write my check out right now because I don't think that there is a horse in my string that can read."

COYOTE SINGIN' SOLO

*If there is one thing I hate, it is a
barking dog at night. I'll lay there
awake and mad until I can't stand
it any longer, get up and poke the
shotgun out the door and blow a
hole in the lawn. A person can
usually get to sleep then, but it
makes the neighbors wonder what
was goin' on.*

*I was gone one time and called the
wife at home. She asked how far
my 30.06 would shoot. I told her
that it all depended on how far she
had it poked up in the air.*

*"Would it shoot clear down to Joe
Harrinton's place?" she asked.
"No," I said. "Why? You and
Joe feudin'?"
"No, but the dogs got to barkin' last
night, and the only gun that was
loaded was your .06, so I stuck it
out the window and shot it off. This
morning Joe came into the store
and said he was out of power
because someone had shot his
transformer, and I was afraid
maybe I did it."*

*I quickly assured her that it
probably was her.*

The coyotes are a singin'.
And now every dog in town,
and every dog on every ranch,
for twenty miles around
is gonna sit and answer them.
They do it every night.
I'm tired, and I want some rest.
It's gonna be a fight.
With eyes as big as saucers,
that keep starin' at the ceilin'.

I know them dogs would shut their face
if they knew how I was feelin'.
And how their owners stand it?
I know they can't sleep through it.
And if they can, I wish they'd share
the secrets, how they do it.
I'd like to get my hands on them:
I'd tighten every collar.
They'd be so busy suckin' air,
they'd cease that bark and holler.
And the coyote left some time ago,
proud of what he's done.
He starts it almost every night,
and he does it just for fun.
But oh, them dogs will keep it up,
and they will, 'till early dawn.
Then they'll lay around the house all day
'cuz they worked hard all night long.
My eyes are red and full of blood.
My lips are tightly curled.
I'm cranky as a pregnant bobcat
with my wrath, not yet unfurled.
Those barks just seem to echo
with my pillow o'er my head.
And my feet are gettin' chilly,
stickin' out the top the bed.
But at last they've drove me crazy.
They've drove me plumb insane.
I'm reachin' for the shotgun.
From the wife, there's no restrain.
'Cuz she knows I have to do it.
Yep, there goes her favorite rose.
Or maybe her pettunnies,
or a chunk of garden hose.
But I let that twelve gauge beller,
and it echoes off the rim.
Startled yips and rattlin' chains,
as them dogs is diggin' in.
It's a universal language,
and almost every mutt agrees,
when buckshot starts a talkin',
it's a thing that they should heed.
My arm is really hurtin',
where my bitin's left it's mark.
And I lay in bed a shakin',

133

waitin' for "just one more bark."
And I'll stay that way 'till morning,
'cuz there ain't no chance of sleep
When that coyote goes to singin',
just outside across the creek.
But it kind of lullaby's me,
'cuz there ain't no chorus follows.
And the singin' of that coyote
echoes up and down the hollows.
My eyes are softly fallin',
as I sink into my pillow.
'Cuz there's nothing more relaxin'
than a coyote singin' solo.

THE PULLING CONTEST

This ole team's the heart of me.
> Their hearts are proud and full.
They work as one together.
> No strangers to hard pulls.
Each new weight's a challenge.
> Each new pull's a test.
There's nothing more fulfilling,
> than to watch them give their best.
And when they've stretched their limits,
> and they've pulled the load they're hauling.
You know that they are champions.
> Hard pulls — their beck and calling.

ASTRADDLE OF BEEF

If you get a calf headed that you are going to doctor by yourself, and he's too big to flank or leg down, and you don't want to bust him or choke him down, here's something that sometimes works. Simply sit on him backwards, slide your butt down until you're sittin' on his neck, and grab a hand full of hair in his flanks. Your weight will bring his head down, and when that happens, throw your weight to one side, and he'll flop on his side – especially if he's moving good.

Note: (This only works on cattle that are not strong enough to hold up your weight with their necks.)

We were working calves through the chute one time, preconditioning them with their shots before we weaned. These calves are weighing over five hundred pounds and have been doing real good. I spotted a bull calf coming towards the chute that must have escaped the knife at brandin' time. I thought to myself that it would be a good time to castrate him, but it would be easier outside on the ground than in the chute. Without saying a word to anyone, I jumped up astraddle of the headcatch and said to turn him out. This calf got up quite a bit of speed before I got properly positioned for the toss. I finally got into position but wasn't dropping his head so much that you would notice. He finally sucked back and went to buckin'. I got under him and got quite a few tracks on me before he turned me go. None of the rest of the crew knew what I was up to at the time, and it tickled them to no end.

"Nice ride, Freckles Brown."

"Things getting a little boring around here, or what?"

It's sure hard to explain to them that if they would just watch, they might just learn something.

THY HEIFER

Once upon a midnight weary,
heifers calvin', weather's dreary.
I stopped to ponder where I was.
My mind is tired and in a fuzz.
I haven't slept for three straight days.
I stumble 'round, my mind a daze.
When all at once what should appear,
but two small eyes, a nose, and ears.
Alas! I cry, where art thy toes?
A soggy glove to blow my nose.
Ye shan't be born, thus unassisted.
I limp around: my knee is twisted.
Straight forth I go for yonder steed.
Come here old friend. You're what I need.
I've got to get yon heifer in.
Up in corner, horse with grin.
Come on old man, I need ya, son.
We don't have time for all your fun.
"You dirty rottin', runnin' snide.
I blessed the day your mother died,"
I calmly say under my breath,
The dungeon and a tortured death.
At last I've got you cornered now.
He faces up— my thoughts to cow.
I place lead rope upon his neck.
My knee goes out. I crash and wreck.
I fall onto his very toes.
He rolls a snort and blows and goes.
I limp back for to get my twine.
This fallen angel will be mine.
He trots right up like long lost friend.
"I'm here to help get heifer in."
I'm sweatin' hard beneath my wraps.
Cold rain is seepin' thru my chaps.
I canter back to maid in need.
In shock I sit on lathered steed.
Before me lies the work of elf.
She's had the damn thing by herself.

FIGHTIN' COWS

The only reason that some cows need to fight with a human is that they think there might be a possibility to reach one. You know, get up close and personal. Chuck tells me of teasing an ole fightin' cow one time and having it backfire.

"Wayne, the boss' son, and I were feedin' with the hired man. Johnny's drivin' a flatbed truck, and we are throwin' off the hay. We're in a big lot, and when we're done, he stops so we can get in the front. Right when we jumped off the truck, this ole cow that likes to fight a little, throws her head in the air and paws at us a couple of times. Being kids, we beller and paw back.

'She won't hurt ya, you chickens, stand yer ground and fight her,' Johnny says.

"At that, we got a little braver and take a few more steps away from the safety of the truck. It isn't long until Wayne and I we're both on our hands and knees, pawin'. We're really tearin' up the sod and bellerin' war. We've got this ole girl's undivided attention, and it isn't long, until here she comes. As we jumped up and turn to scramble on the truck, there it is, gone. Johnny has slipped it into reverse, and let it idle out of the lot.

"It's funny how fast that fun and games can turn into fear and survival."

THE COWBOY

He was made in the West
    where a man's put to test
by the horses and tracks that he's made.
And his love for the land,
    is a thing that is grand.
Life's dues have been hard, but they're paid.

The lessons he's learned
    and the pride that he's earned,
and the knowledge that speaks in his eye
comes from hours in the saddle,
    while he's trotted astraddle,
'tween the land and the good Lord's blue sky.

Through the drought and the flood,
    he's bathed in life's blood.
Life and death seem the stones of his path.
He's seen nature's death,
    put the unfit to rest,
and the love of a cow's newborn calf.

He's been imitated
    'till he's near constipated
by the folks that are faking his part.
They can play 'till they strand,
    but they won't understand
that they're missin' what lives in his heart.

He's got enough sense,
    to take down the fence
that corners most mortal men's minds.
He knows Mother Nature,
    and sure won't forsake Her.
She's twice as hard as she's kind.

And his God, as he knows Him,
    and the things that He shows him,
has taught him one thing for sure.
Mother Nature is hard,
    and you die what you are.
So friend, hope your tracks have been pure.

AN UPSIDE DOWN QUIRTIN'

I've always heard that if you've got a bad one to get on, take him right out in the middle of the biggest patch of rocks that you can find. The horse won't buck near as hard, and you'll ride better than a cocklebur buried in sheep's wool. There might just be some truth to that. I've seen fellers that were bucked plumb out of their saddles, climb back down their mecates and get ahold of something when they saw where they were going to land. I've also seen horses that were sure enough cranky, that you couldn't make buck if they thought that they were going to peel themselves up any. If a feller even wiggled his mustache wrong and that same horse was on good ground, it might be enough to make him blow the cork.

There's a big difference in contest ridin' and ridin' a buckin' horse out were you are going to have to walk twenty miles if you get bedded down. It seems that if a feller got bucked off outside, even if he did have a big rock to break his fall, the limpin' back home and the ribbin' that a guy takes from his counterparts, hurts as much as the fall itself. There isn't much sympathy given on any of the places I ever worked on, unless the person was hurt serious. I mean when I say serious, something that is going to cripple you for a while or maybe even the rest of your life. Bumps, thumps, cuts, bruises, broken fingers, and bad rope burns all fall into the category of wisdom knots.

Some fellers weren't very pretty when it came to ridin' a buckin' horse, but they were damn hard to get on the ground. If a feller was in control and knew that he could get the horse he was ridin' covered, he might set up there with one hand and scratch him a little. But let him get in a storm where mister horse had the upper hand, and you'd see him pull saddle strings, rope strap, and whatever else passed in front of his hands, plumb off his saddle until it looked like a picked chicken.

Some guys weren't ever pretty bronc riders. Audience or none, they rode like a monkey wrestlin' a football. I guess they didn't like the taste of dirt any more than the next guy and would come up with their rope strap every time their horse even stumbled.

I've seen some awful pretty rides in contests, on some very respectable buckin' horses, but the ones that always seem to impress a feller were the good ones "outside." I remember a kid that I used to work with, that had started his kind of tiger striped, shit-muckel dun colored colt. This ole colt was bad to buck, but usually only on good ground. He could buck on the kitchen table and never cover enough ground to fall off. He'd have all four of his feet's tracks on the kitchen ceiling when he was done too.

Jerry had done everything he knew of to talk this ole colt out of buckin', but wasn't having any luck with any of it. He finally decided that the next time he blew up, maybe a good severe quirtin' would change his attitude. Jerry could handle whatever the colt threw at him and was fairly capable of handlin' his quirt too. I was there to see this ole colt get his first taste of it.

We had trotted out from camp that morning right when it was light enough to see. We stopped on top of a little knoll where I was going to scatter my crew. We'd trotted about a mile through the rocks, but for some reason, the very top of this knoll, was cleaner than a tater field. This colt decided that he was loosened up good after that trot and took advantage of this nice ground. On the second jump, down came the quirt, and it wasn't missin'. A couple of jumps later, the string on that quirt broke, and it went flyin' straight into the air. Jerry was goin' through the motions but didn't have his quirt. A couple of spins later, and damned if that quirt didn't come straight back down, and land right in his hand. The only thing different was that this time he had ahold of the popper end. No problem. He just went ahead and gave that colt a little taste of the lead weighted handle.

It was sure pretty watchin' up against that big red sky, with the sun not quite breakin' the far horizon and the morning so fresh and new.

A LITTLE BUCKAROO MEETS SANTA

He took him to the city,
when he was only four.
To do some Christmas shoppin',
in that big department store.

And the sights, they filled his very eyes,
and the smells, they filled his nose.
And everything a goin' on,
kept him right up on his toes.

'Cuz he was just a ranch kid.
This was his first trip to town.
And everything a happenin',
kept him lookin' all around.

Then he finally spotted Santa
at the end of center aisle.
And his little eyes lit right up,
and they sparkled like his smile.

He walked straight on up to Santa,
and he offered his right hand.
Santa took it, and he shook it,
and he thought that that was grand.

He climbed right on up to Santa's knee,
and it was a sure bet
that they was best of buddies,
even though they just had met.

Now, Santa, had a microphone,
and it was wired throughout the store.
And he mentioned 'bout his cowboy boots,
and that big black hat he wore.

But when he called him, "cowboy"
the conversation was all through.
"I ain't no cowboy, mister,
just a God-damned buckaroo."

I'M ALL DONE NOW

A feller that worked for me one time, related this story about a kid that he knew:

He was fairly forked and takin' on some cranky horses to ride. I pulled into the yard to visit this ole kid, and he's just ready to get on this big grey horse. I asked him what he was, and he told me that he didn't know too much about him. He'd just got him, and all he knew was that he had some age on him, and he's supposed to buck a little.

By the look in this ole pony's eye, I thought that it might be worth watchin'. The kid steps on and finds out right away that everything that he's heard about the horse is true. The horse is big and strong, and he doesn't get a chance to get sat down very good before he's in a storm. He's bucked off, right from the get go, but the ole horse just keeps pickin' him up. He's grabbin' at anything that passes by in front of him and stays with him for quite a few jumps. Finally, his feet are stickin' straight in the air, and his head is along side of the horses neck. In a voice that could have come out of "granny's rocker," he looks at me and calmly says, "I'm all done now."

BALDY (DIED IN THE SPRING)

Although this didn't actually happen to me, it has
happened to a lot of people. I've had that "empty in the
gut" feeling when I've went out to catch a horse and
found some old favorite sound asleep stretched out in
the sunshine.

It was one of those really bright April mornings. You
know the kind. The smell of new just hangs around in
various shades of growin'. The sun is so warm on your back
that you have to stop for just a second and let it sink clear
into your heart. You can always tell when it sinks clear in
because your eyes light up a little, and your mouth turns up
at the corners. You get to lookin' at the horizon instead of
what you have been stumbling over all winter.

The kind of day that makes you feel like shedding your
coat and rollin' in the sand, knockin' off any ole warbles and
any ole shades of winter.

The kind of day that makes you glad you didn't winter-kill.

It was on just such a day that I was headed down to the
barn to grain old Baldy. Now, Baldy was an old cowhorse that
I'd had pensioned for about the last seven years. He was a
fine old friend and a gentleman. Baldy was taking advantage
of this warm sunshine too. He's just stretched out in it,
soakin' up the rays.

I whistle at him to come have some breakfast. Baldy
doesn't even twitch an ear. I holler at him and rattle that
grain bucket. Baldy doesn't move.

Then that cold empty feelin' comes crawlin' up the back
of my neck, raisin' all the hair as it goes. It finally reaches it's
peak and spreads over my very soul, like oil on cold water. It
settles empty in my stomach and holds it there in it's clutch.
In a voice that's empty and small, I ask, "Baldy?"

I guess that I already knew the answer, but it takes
reality just a second to break fear's barrier and sink in. Baldy
was gone. I wrote this poem:

Why is it that they fight the wind,
 the bitter cold and snow?
Then just as spring is turnin' green,
 they up and just let go.
They hump around all winter.
 You treat 'em to your best.
Then just as spring is turnin' green,
 they take that last long rest.
I've seen it happen lots of times,
 to horses, beasts, and man.
I guess winter's not for travelin'.
 I guess it's in God's plan.

CANNED ON THE OUTHOUSE

We had an outfit leased one time where the cattle were on the outside on a winter range situation. During this time, we had to haul water. Some places had wells, but for the most part, the water was hauled to troughs. It took one, full time man, to watch over the watering of these cows. Beings though there wasn't much cowboying to be done, the feller that was hired, usually had lots of spare time and was paid accordingly. I've found through life that you usually get what you pay for.

This particular winter, Dad had hired an artist. This artist was a highly educated man when it came to books and vocabulary, but he didn't know "sick 'em" about the cattle industry or about cow camps.

We moved out to camp to gather the cattle right before they started calving. They stayed "inside" then, until they moved to their spring range. When this happened, the hired man was moved into the little bunkhouse, and our family moved into the little trailer.

The trailer was completely over ran with mice, and there were birds in different stages of decay, hanging on the walls. These birds were models for his artwork, and the whole trailer had an unpleasant odor. Mom told him that she didn't care if he kept them or not, but that they were going outside.

Dad wasn't very pleased about the way this man had kept camp up, but he had done a decent job of keeping water in front of all of the cows. Mom, on the other hand, was a little more than upset.

The first morning, when the hired man came in for breakfast, my sister was dumping a couple of mice out of some traps that she had set the night before.

"What am I going to tell them?" the man asked.

"Tell who, what?" Sis asked.

"Why, all of their little brothers and sisters and cousins," was his answer.

"Tell 'em that some make it and some don't," said Sis.

It wasn't long before we were saddled and ready to go start gathering cows. The hired man's horse took objection to the way he drug his foot over his rump when he got on and took a couple of little jumps. Immediately, he dropped the reins and grabbed the saddle horn with both hands. After it was all over, he said, pointing to the horn, "I had no inclination to grab – what's the terminology of this banister handle anyway?"

In a few days, we had everything gathered, and we were working the first-calf heifers off of the older cows. Dad was bringing them down an alley, hollering "in and by." About half way through, the artist threw the gate open and let things mix. He told my dad to stop yelling at him. Dad explained that he wasn't hollering at him, but more at the cows and was just making sure that he was heard.

Everything was going along again, fairly smooth, when all of a sudden, he threw the gate open and let things mix again. He told Dad that he was sure that he was yelling at him. Dad hadn't been, but he was now.

"See that outhouse over there? Go sit on it with the door open and watch. Maybe you can learn something. Better yet, go roll your bed. You're fired!" Dad yelled.

At this, the hand came to the trailer where mom had been watching the whole affair, and said, "Your husband seems to want to terminate my employment here."

"Oh? Sometimes he gets a little testy when he's working cows. The best thing for you to do is to go right back out there and make sure it's final," Mom said, with a little sparkle in her eye.

Straight back out to Dad he heads to see if that's really what Dad wants to do. When he left the corral that time, there was absolutely no doubt. Even my sister and I learned a few new words that day. It was one of those times when you were just a kid that you couldn't laugh, no matter how hard you might want to.

147

A NIGHT ON THE TOWN

It's Saturday night,
    and I'm scrubbin' me down.
'Cuz it's time that I had me
    a night on the town.
I've been in this camp now
    for sixty five days,
and it's time that I showed
    all the girls how to play.

I'll go to the barber,
    for clippin' and trimmin'.
A night on the town boys,
    that's how it's beginnin'.
I'll go to the bank,
    for to cash my pay check.
Then I'll buy some new clothes
    and a hat, what the heck.

I'll get me a room,
    and I'll get me some grub.
Then I'll have a few toddies
    in some quiet club.
And when they remove me,
    outside on my ear,
I'll know that it's time
    to shift up to high gear.

I'll head to another,
    one more aptly suited,
for fellers and fillies,
    that's hatted and booted.
Where whoopin' and hollers
    are normally found.
The fun's just beginnin' –
    a night on the town.

To a place that's got music,
    a night full of dance.
The girls'll be there,
    and there might be a chance
for to find one I like.
    I'll be debonaire.

How can she refuse,
     when I offers a chair?

Now this is more like it.
     There's music and women.
My kind of bar.
     The fun's just beginnin'.
As I step through the door,
     I'm met with a smile
from the prettiest thing
     that I've seen for a while.

Her face sort of blushes
     when I stops on her glance.
I sure smile back
     and ask her to dance.
She's warm and she's friendly,
     and smiles oh, so sweet.
She's as good as there is boys,
     and light on her feet.

The dance is now ending
     as I'm trying to think.
But the words never come,
     so I give her a wink.
Her face just turns red,
     and she gives a warm smile.
I thank her quite kindly
     and walk her that mile

to the chair where she's sittin',
     with some of her friends.
It's one of those nights
     that I hope never ends.
Well, what do you know,
     some old friends of mine
up there at the bar
     that I worked with one time.

So we catch up on gossip
     and what we've been doin'.
The broncs that we've rode,
     bad horses we're shoein'.
What outfits we're workin'.
     Whose iron's in the fire.

Good grass and bad water.
Snow storms and mud mire.

The first thing you know,
it's a quarter past four.
The place has died down;
they're sweepin' the floor.
We're the only ones left,
the same story to tell.
The girls all went home.
Back to camp. Just as well.

So I'll save up my money,
my time, and my pain.
And maybe next time,
I'll at least get her name.

UNCLE LEO'S INSTANT DOGS

Every since the first of time,
    when wolf was domesticated,
man has tried to prove his dog.
    Some loved, some dearly hated.

And every one's a "gooder"
    if you're talkin' to his master.
But, let him take his dog and leave,
    the air might turn to laughter.

But I think I've finally found a way
    to end this age old battle.
The one that always does come up,
    with horses, dogs, and cattle.

I went down to the local pound,
    and picked all kinds and gender.
I took them home and ground them up,
    and threw them in a blender.

Then dried and fried and hydro-pried,
    and into that compactor,
I threw in, "Bring 'em back", and "Head 'em".
    All essential factor.

And out they came, by fifties
    like little crayon logs,
in little pocket packets –
    "Uncle Leo's Instant Dogs."

And all's you need is water,
    to bring 'em back to form.
They'll run for twenty minutes
    or until they get too warm.

But when they dry completely out?
    They just poof into powder.
It seems to me the perfect way.
    Sure saves on puppy chowder.

And if you need another,
    simply soak another log.

And standin', waitin' for commands,
    is another "Instant Dog."

Now they worked good in the swamplands,
    and in the Everglades.
In all the lush green pastures
    that the irrigators made.

But out here on the desert,
    and in the drier parts,
it seems them dogs was poofin'
    before they got a start.

Now cowboys don't haul that extra weight
    on them 'outside circles' that they make.
So they just get up two hours early.
    Drink more coffee. Makes 'em squirrely.

So when you're out there miles from camp.
    It's so damn dry, your spit ain't damp.
And when you need a mutt, "Doggone it,"
    think again and say, "Piss on it."

THE BEAR STORY

I was in a bar one time when I heard a friend of mine who had been logging up in Montana, telling this story to a girl. The funniest part was, this ol' gal is believing what Patty is telling her.

"Well, you know I've been up in Montana logging, and they tell me to watch out for grizzly bears. I guess they'd lost a couple of good fellers just the week before I'd started. Well, I fall trees for two weeks without even seeing one. But I had seen some pretty fresh tracks, and by the size of the feet on this ole bear, I can tell he's a big one.

"I went out the next morning, and it was just like all the rest. I had been falling hard all morning and had just made the undercut in another tree when my saw ran out of gas. I had just sat my saw down and headed for my gas can when I hear this old bear a charging me through the brush. I forget about the gas and climbed the tree that I'd been working on. I'd always heard that a grizzly won't climb a tree and that must be right because that old bear stops when he gets to the bottom of my tree. I can tell he's really upset that he didn't get me by the way he keeps glaring at me. He just keeps swaying back and forth, shifting his weight from one side to the other. By the way he's a-talking, I know he's disappointed.

"Pretty soon he stands on his hind legs and starts pushing that tree back and forth, a-hoping to shake me out of its top. He's giving it a pretty good whipping, but I'm not turning loose for nothing, and he soon realizes it. He gets down on all fours and walks around the tree. When he sees that undercut, it's just like the lights come on, and he grabs my saw and tries to start it.

"Now that was one smart bear, but he isn't smart enough to put more gas in that saw. He throws it down and starts shaking the tree again. He soon gives that up and just sits down and glares in disgust. I'm sure hoping he doesn't think of the gas. He sits there for a little while longer, then heads off in the direction of the creek.

"I give him about an hour to be sure he's gone before I head out of the top of that tree. Well, I'm just about out when I hear that bear coming again. Straight back to the top I go.

"When I look down, there stands that grizzly again. He's got a beaver under each arm, and says, 'You're comin' out of that tree this time you Irish s.o.b!'"

PRAYER FOR RAIN

Lord, we sure need moisture here.
    The land is gettin' parched.
The grass is turnin' dry and brown,
    and where the cattle've marched
back and forth to water-holes,
    that now too are givin' in.
The alkali dust is powder dry
    and hangs there in the wind.
The sky is blue as blue can be.
    There ain't no clouds nowhere.
Lord, we sure need moisture here.
    Make it rain, so we can share
with all your other creatures,
    no mind to kind or size.
All's I ask is hurry, Lord,
    'fore all us creatures die.

THE QUARTER HORSE

There's legends in the Quarter Breed,
 the old foundation sires.
They were picked for speed and quickness.
 Had the traits that it requires,
to run a short race, quickly.
 They were mostly picked for speed.
Had a certain conformation,
 no matter what the breed.
Now before you get to thinkin',
 that I'm puttin' this breed down,
I think that they're the ticket.
 There's no better horse around.
For the things that we are doin',
 and the way we work today,
the Quarter Horse is sure on top.
 He sure does earn his hay.
All's that I am sayin'
 is if you trace him far enough,
you'll find that he's a mixture –
 just not pure-blood Quarter stuff.
He might go back to Thoroughbred
 or have some Percheron blood.
Joe Hancock's, Mama's daddy,
 was a purebred Percheron stud.
And in the nineteen forty's,
 everybody knew Barbra B.
But, her grandad, B'ar Hunter,
 in parenthesis, has (TB).
Three Bars, Top Deck, Depth Charge,
 though all three sires are dead,
were legends in the Quarter Breed.
 Registered Thoroughbred.
So you see, it is a mixture
 of traits, that made the breed.
They changed the horse, for better,
 and were mostly picked for speed.
So legends bred the fastest mares,
 and speed was what they sought.
But crosses, sometimes don't work out,
 and speed isn't what they got.
You take the likes of Doc Bar,
 and we know that he was fine,
but it's said amongst the racin' world,

he couldn't outrun a fat porcupine.
But you know that he was "cowy,"
    and he built a dynasty.
In the reinin' and the cuttin',
    he plumb changed the industry.
But at last, I've found a pureblood.
    He's gentle and he's kind.
He sits outside of Safeway.
    One quarter, at a time.

C&B FEEDLOT

I was working at a feedlot one winter, just riding pens for sick cattle and processing new cattle. One of the fellers that I rode pens with in those days stayed on and is now managing the whole operation. This is a story about him, when he was just like the rest of the guys, "riding pens".

Now anyone who hasn't been around a feedlot in the winter, I'd say, is pretty lucky. As far as working conditions go, to say the least, it can get, let's say, mighty sticky. This winter had been a lot wetter than normal, and I don't know if it was any stickier or not, but it sure was deeper. The sticky places in some spots was clear up to your horse's belly and not a good place for a weak mount. Now this ol' kid that I'm riding pens with is on a three year old colt he's starting. A nice colt, but just not grown up enough to be real strong yet. We were working a sick steer out of a pen one morning when it happened.

The ole steer is having a hard time seeing the hole, and Eric is trying to get him bent on the fence and bring him back up towards the gate. He just gets his speed up when his horse hit a low spot in the pen. Now these low spots are hard to see because just like the ocean, the surface stays fairly level. The bottom isn't always constant. His colt just isn't strong enough to pull on through it and goes down. It kind of catches E.J. unsuspecting and really launches him. Him and the colt both go plumb under.

The colt gets up and goes to a corner in the pen, but Eric just stays down. I ride over to see if I can find him.

Pretty soon, this form starts to appear out of this sea of green dough. With a closer look, I can see that it's Eric. It's hard to make him out as a human until he takes off his hat and wipes his eyes. He reminds me of a raccoon that I saw bogged down in a spring one time. The only part of him that had stayed above surface was one brand new yellow cotton glove.

"Could I get you to pull me out?" he asks. "I'm stuck on the bottom, and to get up, I'm going to have to get this brand new glove all dirty."

I hated to tell him no, but my old horse isn't seeing him for what he really is, and if I threw him my rope, I was afraid he might drop it. After I found out that he wasn't hurt, there wasn't anything going to make me step off to help him.

"No, you don't look very sanitary to be touching. Either the glove gets dirty, or you sit there and die. I'll go gather up your horse." I said laughing.

"Augh, here goes." And with that he dropped his new yellow glove and pried himself off of the bottom. I brought him his horse, but he never does get back on. He just wades out of the pen, and heads off up the feed alley towards the vet-shack. Just before I turn the garden hose on him, he sticks his head into the vet shack and tells the boss, "I've got to go home for a few minutes. I think I've just chit my pants."

LINE DANCIN'

*This poem was the result of when
Chuck Messner and I went to a
guides' convention in Eugene, OR. A
few of the other guides from Eastern
OR and ourselves spent a week, one
night in a bar called the Rockin'
Rodeo.*

*I must first introduce this poem with
reference to the word synchronization.
To most, synchronization is easily
related to line dancers, drill teams,
cheerleaders, etc. To a cattle minded
person, synchronization is a process
used in artificial insemination. A small
hormonal implant is placed into the
female cattle to bring them all in
estrus in a short period of time. With
the Artificial Insemination Technician
in mind, I do my "Line Dancin'" poem.*

Well, I'd never really been out West,
'till I went there this last spring.
To a bar called the "Rockin' Rodeo",
in the (cowtown?) of Eugene.

Now some ole Holstein cow had died.
A kid made her into chaps.
And on every head was a George Strait hat,
anchored with a "Cinderella Strap."

The barmaids had "Jose Cuervo,"
one holstered on either hip.
And the bouncers wore leather dusters.
Hot sweat drippin' off their lips.

I figured we were pickin' partners,
as I stepped in through the door.
I was standin' with about fifteen fellers,
them fillies lined up 'cross the floor.

When all at once, the music broke
race horses from the gate.

And me, a-not expectin' it,
'o course I breaks out late.

But I heads across the dance floor.
I'm a bringin' up the field
when them fellers all came over me.
There weren't no stop sign or yield.

But, I'd been around enough to know
that somethin' spooked 'em bad.
So I turns around and ran,
the way them fellers all just had.

Then just like a flight of blackbirds,
just like they'd all been "keyed",
they spins around. So I'm thinkin',
now I'm the one that's in the lead.

And them fillies are prancin' to us.
And I'm in the winnin' spot
when they all turn their backs on me.
My luck, damned if not.

Then they go to scrapin' off their boot.
So I goes right to guessin'
that someone's had a dog out there,
and he's been out there messin'.

Then they do a skip and jump;
they're sure a steppin' light.
Then they go to scrapin' off their other boot,
so I figures I was right.

Then I get to lookin'.
Hell, they're doin' this in time.
Just a hoppin' and a boppin',
and a dancin' in a line.

And I'm feelin' pretty lonesome.
Feelin' like some centerpiece.
While everybody's laughin'
as I prods along my feet.

Then just like some snuffy Brangus cow,
I sees a place to be.

It might need a little widenin',
but that's the place for me.

So I breaks that line of dancers.
I was headed for fresh air.
When I see my partner laughin',
near to fall out of his chair.

So we sits down and watches.
Maybe has a drink or two.
And we kind of talked it over,
and I'm not certain that it's true.

But the way them city "country folks"
has all been "synchronized,"
it didn't take us very long,
'till we full realized;

if all them heifers come in at once,
it weren't no place to toy.
So we got up a leavin',
knowin' it was no place for a boy.

Spring of '88

*This poem came from a bad wreck with a bunch of
cattle that I ran on farm circles one winter and spring.
I've noticed that ranchers and farmers don't
necessarily have anywhere near the same priorities. To
make a long story short, I was finally forced down to
seven circles of alfalfa that would be starting their
second year of production. I had the first cutting of hay
off of them the prior year bought, and had been
supplementing the cattle on the corn circles with it. The
spring broke early that year, and instead of planting
beans like was the original plan, they decided to plant
wheat instead. They disced up my "room" in just a
couple of days and left me standing on those alfalfa
circles. It was just starting to grow a little, and I
thought I had numbers enough to keep ahead of it. No
such luck. In about a week's time, I had 2500 head of
baby pairs and really heavy cows, divided up on three
125 acre circles. In another week, I had all of the cattle
fenced on brush corners off the alfalfa. The trouble
came by having to be next door to that rapidly growing
alfalfa with nothing but a hot wire in between.*

*It seemed that the cattle that got in trouble the fastest
the last week that we were still on the circles were the
cows due to calve in the next week or two. I guess with
that full term calf in there, they just didn't have enough
room to accommodate any gas. I had only lost one cow
that week, but had doctored several for bloat, and it
had me pretty spooked.*

*I had about 500 of my heaviest cows in one circle and
was working pairs out as they would calve and
working heavies into them about once a week. By this
time the alfalfa fields all were about six inches high
and growing fast. I checked them several times a day,
and I was hoping to get a couple of more weeks out of
that country to let a little grass start at home which
was at a much higher elevation.*

*One afternoon, I let my crew go early. One person
stayed, and we were going to put our heavies to bed
and call it a day. About that time, a big front blew in,
and the wind started blowing about fifty miles per hour.*

When we got to their brush lot it was empty and the cows were all in the alfalfa and in trouble. I sent that person back to camp hopin' to catch some of the crew still there and then hustle back to help me. I almost had the cows back into their lot when she showed up again. The last cow off the alfalfa went down just as she entered the lot. I got off and stuck her while Sandy tried to get some "Thera-bloat" down her. "I think she's dead," she said. "Well, get back on and catch one that not. We're in serious trouble here."

It was only a matter of minutes until my crew showed up, but only my wife and I were experienced enough ropers to get one headed. With the wind blowing so hard, you could only rope going with the wind. Every time you would turn one up, you'd have to ride around two dead ones to catch another. Before I went to bed, some three days later, we'd lost 45 head.

I left Billie to run the crew and ship out the heavy cows first, then she paired up loads of baby pairs and shipped them. Out of the six or seven hundred head of baby pairs she shipped out that week, I remember that they only shipped one cow and calf back. The rest were straight. Thank God for her and the crew.

All the time that she and the crew were doing that, I continuously circled those cattle. We had put up a second wire on all of the fences, which ended up being a big mistake. The big tumble weeds would roll over one wire, but would get tangled in two, and pull down the fence. It didn't take too long to change that. Also if one of those big weeds would hit one of the fiber glass posts, the fence would go down. When things finally settled down enough to reflect, I wrote this poem for those cows.

They died like flies in '88.
They trod a path through Heaven's gate.
And there they found a place to graze
With trees and shelter, to lie and laze.
Abundant grass for them to eat.
Not dry corn stalks and regrowth wheat.
No fences there. No dry-lot pens.
No chutes to be ran through and ran through again.
They drank their water from a bubbling brook.
No more to stand and bawl and look
and wonder where the truck was now
that hauled water to those Earthly cows.
They got their minerals from the land.
Not fertilizers leached out through the sand.
They roamed at will as the seasons changed.
A peaceful place that they now ranged.
And not one single truck be found.
No more to be rammed and jammed around.
Those poor ole girls sure earned their peace.
God, tell me it's owned and not just leased.

THE WOOD-PILE BLUES

I was just a kid, working on my first job away from home, when the boss tells me this story as we're gassing up the pickup one day.

"I guess I must have been about your age when this happened," Barry tells me. "Back in them days, we didn't have these electric gas pumps or big gravity flow tanks, and we had to gas everything by hand out of fifty gallon barrels. They didn't deliver then. I'd just got done filling up my rig when my father came drivin' up in his brand new pickup. I knew that he was going to ask me to fill it, so I hurried up, pulled mine forward, and lit up a cigarette. When he got out, he tells me that I'm not done pumping yet, so I headed back over and started to fill his.

'Put that damned cigarette out, before you blow us both up.'

"I must have not got it stepped on very good because when I spilled the gas over, it sure caught on fire. Dad sure got excited and threw that pickup into reverse to get away from all of those gas barrels. Not really caring or looking where he was going, he got into too big a hurry, and backed up onto the woodpile until he was high centered. It burned up about ten cords of wood that we'd just gathered for the coming winter, along with his brand new pickup.

"I had to go get more wood all by myself. It was a big job, but at least I was away from Dad for a few days."

CAMP FIRES

An ember sprang from the fire's ring
    and almost broke the trance.
As we all sat 'round, with wisdom eyes,
    and watched the flames at dance.
Cross legged there, with minds at ease,
    all with hollow gaze.
Self wisdom shown in every face,
    as we watched the embers blaze.
And though the camp is seven strong,
    each man's at his own.
Each man to his journey.
    Each man holds a throne.
Each man dreams his dream alone.
    Not a single word is said.
The only sound is the fire's song.
    As the dreamers all are led
to a place that has no meaning,
    to a place of inner peace.
And only when the fire dies down,
    does this peaceful dreaming cease.
Then, one by one, each man gets up
    and drifts off to his bed,
feeling somewhat wiser,
    Like his soul has just been fed.
A filter for the mind, perhaps,
    as it holds you in it's trance,
but it happens every time you sit,
    and watch the camp fire dance.

CHRISTMAS '89

One morning, we caught horses
    for to gather in a late cow
that had somehow missed the gather in the fall.
And the cold snow, it was squealin'
    as hay wagon went a wheelin',
as we fed the other critters, one and all.

Except for one ole sister.
    Makes me wonder how we missed her.
Some trapper, he had seen her way up high.
And we knew we had to hurry
    'cuz the weather made us worry.
One more good snow, and she would surely die.

You'd a thought she would have had sense,
    for to drift on down the drift fence.
The gates are open all the way below.
But no, she's got to mess around
    till there's lots of ice and frozen ground,
and horses to their bellies in the snow.

Well, the morning chores are done here.
    So we gathers up the pack gear,
and manties up a couple bales of hay,
for the trail will be a rough one.
    Drifts up there aren't gonna be fun.
But she will eat, if we don't get her all the way.

As we head up ever higher,
    for to save this poor ole dier,
we trade at breakin' trail in the snow.
Makes me wonder if we'll do it?
    Will we even make it through it?
The deep snow makes the goin' mighty slow.

There hasn't been much talkin'
    as the horses keep on walkin'.
Don't go far until they have to catch their air.
And their breath and sweat is steamin',
    and they wonder what we're dreamin'
that would ever make us want to go up there.

But at least it isn't snowin',
    and the wind ain't started blowin'.
And we hope it doesn't start 'till we get out.
And the snow is gettin' deep now.
    Still a mile to go to that cow.
Kind of let the horses pick out their own route.

As we head on down the hillside,
    to the bottom where this ole hide
is supposed to be a livin' solitaire,
I thought I heard a calf bawl.
    Could of swore I heard a calf bawl.
And the first thing that I do is start to swear.

'Cuz if there's one thing I don't want,
    it's a baby calf on this jaunt.
Tough enough upon a critter fully grown.
And I know she's in a tough shape,
    not much to eat, 'cept snowflakes.
Her water's froze. A cold north wind's been blowin'.

But, through all my agitation,
    I must stand in admiration
of the way this cow has tended to her young.
He's tucked up in a cut-bank cave,
    just lies and hears the winter rave,
the way his little barn is over-hung.

And the cow's not lookin' too bad,
    for no more to eat than she's had.
But we break a bale and let the party feed.
Then we build us up a rough sled.
    Even has a baby calf bed.
I think that we'll come up with all we need.

Now, we're ready for the trip back,
    to the feed-ground and our warm shack.
I think that I'll just set the packhorse free.
Ma will take the calf in tow,
    the cow will follow, mooin' low –
The packhorse, Ma, the calf, the cow, and me.

As we break out on the ridge top,
    and we take another rest stop,
we can see the lights of our camp, far below.

And the cow just keeps on mooin',
  kind of soft like, more like cooin'
'cuz she loves that little guy we've got in tow.

As we ride on through the moonlight,
  makes us feel as if we've done right
even though the temperature has dropped right down.
And if it isn't too late,
  when we ride in through that yard gate,
we'll still make Christmas dinner there in town.

JONNY'S LAST DAY

A good friend of mine that I worked with one time was a pretty good bronc peeler. Jonny told me this story about an outfit that he had worked on a few years earlier.

" This outfit had some fairly tough horses, and I was getting by them all pretty good except for one. It seems that every time this ol' horse came up in my string, I was going to get a mouth full of dirt. He just had my number. It usually happened when I first got on, but that wasn't always the case. Sometimes I might have been riding hard all day and something would set him off. He was always aware of when you were just a little bit out of where you should be and wasn't above taking advantage of a situation.

"I had worked there for over a year and was thinking about moving on, but I had made up my mind that I was going to get that horse covered just once before I left. It happened on one of those winter mornings when it was about twenty below zero.

"The rest of the boys were already mounted, and we had decided to give this ole horse a good beating while he was bucking. Right on schedule the action starts.

"He let me get completely on and sat down for the first time since I started riding him, then he took to me. I was tapped off, and I knew I had him rode this time. All of a sudden, the damnedest storm of quirts and romals you ever saw came out of the sky from all directions. I don't think that any of them ever landed on the horse, but they sure beat me on my poor froze to death hands. I knew that if one of the boys ever does hit the horse, it's gonna sting him bad.

"He bucked up to a board gate on the corral that we had just closed behind us and couldn't figure out which way to turn. He finally turned up between this fence and the barn. Now, the rafters of this old barn stuck out over the top of the fence, and it wasn't a place that you would have led a gentle bridle horse. The only consolation that I have, is that the boys won't follow, and they quit thumping on my hands.

"I broke the first rafter with my forehead, and I start getting loose. I can't leave because every time I come up, a rafter drives me back into the saddle. By the time we got out from under the eaves of that barn, the horse had quit bucking. I was peeled up pretty good, but I called it a qualified ride and gave the boss my notice that night."

IT'S HOME FOR A BUCKAROO

I was born in a sea of sagebrush,
    and I'm livin' for what I do.
'Cuz this country was made for a mama cow,
    and it's home for a buckaroo.
And there's lots that some won't think pretty,
    'Cuz it's covered with brush and rock.
But it fits the needs of a buckaroo,
    and his herds of parent livestock.
For to keep this nation supplied in beef,
    and to keep all the feed-lots full.
Someone has to raise that calf.
    And that starts with a cow and a bull.
And this range ain't much good for a yearlin'.
    Least wise, if you're lookin' for weight.
So the mama cow gets the nod in the spring
    when you turn 'em out the home-yard gate.
And she'll scratch out a livin', out there on the range
    and hopefully bring in son or daughter.
And hopefully they weigh good, but that all depends
    on the weather, the grass, and the water.
For the country is rough, and the country is tough,
    and it makes for a hardy crew.
In good times and bad – these dry years are sad –
    it's home for a buckaroo.

FOR ROANY, THE MILK COW

They say that you can't love a cow
 like you do a dog or horse.
But what I've got to do tonight
 fills my heart with great remorse.
For you've raised two score of children,
 all five neighbors' plus my own.
You've had twelve little ones yourself,
 and every one's been roan.
Plus every year, some extras,
 that some heifer wouldn't feed.
You've loved 'em like they were your own
 and gave 'em what they'd need.
Every kitten purred to you
 to hurry and get through.
So they could circle 'round their dish,
 like little barn cats do.
I've sat that stool for twelve straight years
 with my brow 'ginst your warm hide.
I damned near drowned you with my tears,
 the day our Jimmy died.
You know, ole girl, I've told you things
 I couldn't a told the wife.
I love you like you were my kin.
 You've been part of my life.
'Cuz cows like you don't come around
 but once in a million years.
My heart is full of sorrow,
 and my eyes are full of tears.
But now you're down and dyin',
 and I know what must be done.
I'm chokin' on my very heart
 as I raise my tremblin' gun.
I pray to God to take you home.
 I pray that I don't miss.
I send my love forever.
 And I squeeze the "Nosler's Kiss."
Your hollow eyes glaze over;
 my heart sinks to the dregs.
I turn with guts up in my throat
 and sink on dispaired legs.

We buried her next morning,
    out under her shade tree.
May the sweet grass always fill you,
    and your soul be always free.

IS GEORGINE HOME?

It seemed like the "greenhorn" Irishmen in this country loved to fight. This story was told about one such incident.

We were doing a little drinking one night as one of us had come across a bottle of whiskey. It was dark out, and we were passing the bottle and visiting. All at once, the bottle came up missin'.

"Has anyone seen me quart of whiskey?"

"I'm not for certain, lad, but I think it just left under the care of George. He headed for home."

"That's no good. 'Tis no good at all. I better go and save us some."

At that, he headed straight to the house in question, and knocked loudly on the door. George's wife came to the door. "Good evenin', mum. Is Georgine in?"

"No. Georgine isn't home."

"I'll have a look for me self, mum," and he walked straight into their bedroom, to find George asleep and the quart of whiskey right beside him on the dresser. He soon came out to those who were anxiously awaiting his return.

"How did it go, man? Were you able to find the whiskey?"

"Aye, I have it now. The devil had it right along side of him, and was sound asleep."

"Well, what did you do?"

"Why, I lifted him by his fringe, and gave him a few good stout pokes right in the puss, I did."

BULL SLIPPERS

I guess if I have a signature poem, this would have to be it. Everyone knew my feet before they knew my name. I wear these silly little slippers when I recite this poem and have a little routine that I do as I recite it. As far as where the poem got its start, Billie and I were camped with the cows on the corn circles for the second winter. My sister sent me the slippers as a Christmas gift. I was sitting in the ole recliner one evening and was wearing my new slippers. It wasn't long before they started fighting. Before I could get a handle on them, they were up chasing Billie around the trailer. The rest is history.

Sis gave me slippers for Christmas.
    A thoughtful gift I thought.
They were hairy and horned and had a ring in their nose.
    Horned Herefords, damned if not.
I slipped into 'em easy,
    like I was slippin' on some bronc.
I tried 'em out real easy,
    then we headed for a honky-tonk.
We were strollin' down the sidewalk,
    feelin' like some purebred breed.
And them two little critters
    just kept switchin' for the lead.
We brushed up, just for a second,
    checked my watch at the ole lamp-pole.
But I felt 'em break into a trot
    as we neared that water-hole.
Now I let 'em take on quite a soak,
    for I knowed it'd been a spell.
How long they'd been in that dry-lot box?
    Well, it was pretty hard to tell.
About then, from the outside, in come a heifer.
    Just as purty as could be.
And I thought them critters might 'ave been steers,
    but I was wrong, that's plain to see.
I tried my best to hold 'em back,
    but I could see I was losin' ground.
Wasn't long before they jumped the fence,
    reached that heifer in a single bound.
Now she didn't seem real impressed at first,
    by the way we rushed right in.

Then I saw her look down at my feet.
   And I thought I saw her grin.
She was lookin' down at them,
   and they returned the stare.
She said, "Why's your toes a twitchin?"
   Damned bulls was a testin' the air!
While they held her eyes in ponder,
   well, I kinda hid my chew.
And I asked her if she'd like to dance?
   It was the least that I could do.
An unpredicted tragedy.
   A terrible mistake.
Them bulls, they took to fightin',
   just as soon as we cracked the gate.
Around and around the room we went,
   a crashin' into chairs.
And when them two fellers locked their horns,
   they didn't have a care.
Well, they damned near had me winded,
   when the left one broke and ran.
I thought that I'd been drug to death
   when we ran on through that band.
With the help of a deputy sheriff,
   and the local pet control,
they finally got the cuffs on me,
   then they took them bulls in tow.
Now it's thirty days in this ole cell,
   and I'm tired of their bologna.
When I get 'em home, I'm gonna dehorn 'em,
   and whittle on their cahonnies.

YOU'VE GOT THE BIG GUN

A buyer came through our country one fall and put together a load of yearlings that weren't shipped with the rest of the yearling cattle that fall. Mostly calves that might have been lame at that time or had a bad eye or just didn't fit in too well with the other cattle at the time most of the yearlings left the country. These cattle came from three or four outfits and were just a mixed batch of odds and ends.

The driver had a bit of bad luck about thirty miles from where these cattle were loaded and tipped the truck over. It just happened to be along a summer pasture of ours that was quite a willow patch. The wreck killed three or four, crippled several others, and totally spooked what was left.

After a few days of gathering, all but a couple were accounted for, either rounded up or found dead from injuries sustained in the wreck. The buyer told us to keep an eye out for them, and if they were crippled up too bad, to put them out of their misery, but to keep him up to date on what we were finding.

In about a week, we found one down in the thickest part of the willows. This yearling had a bad broken leg, and a much worse disposition. On the way home that night, two of the crew went to the willow patch to put her down. Tommy was armed with a small caliber pistol, while Jerry had a high powered rifle. As they slid down the steep hill and into the willows, all hell broke loose. They came out faster than they went in, with this fever crazed heifer blowing snot in their hip pockets.

The heifer seemed to read the odds and stayed on the tracks of the feller packing the pistol. It seemed for a minute that she might over take ole Tommy and even those odds a little.

She was gaining ground as the hill started taking its toll. Tommy started shooting over his shoulder and yelling at Jerry, "Where the hell are you going? You've got the big gun, and this ain't no meat hunt."

Looking back after the dreaded deed had been done, Tom says, "Good thing you shot when you did. I was running short on bullets, and I was damned sure running short on wind."

179

SATAN AND JUDE

This is based on a true story that
was told to me by Doug Shook.
Doug worked for me when we
were up in Northern Oregon. He
was sure good help and a lot of
fun to work with. He was the
teamster in this poem and said it
turned out pretty close to what
really happened.

It was in the spring of '72;
I'd just got out of school.
I was young and tough and brawny.
No kid for Sunday School.

I decided'd I'd hit it out alone,
the family was a fight.
So I got a job a pitchin' hay,
and on the "Ox Bow" I did light.

Now, I'd heard they fed with horses,
and that's all that filled my dreams.
And I was surely anxious to work
one of them big ole gentle teams.

But what I thought, and what I got,
had different magnitude.
They led me out a "bronco team."
One named Satan. One named Jude.

And I knew I had my hands full
by the way the boss explained,
quite carefully the "does and don'ts."
This team weren't all that tame.

"Never leave the wagon,
unless you take along a line.
'Cuz this ole pair of ponies,
has left several men behind.

"Always tie 'em solid
when you're loadin' up with hay.

They'll kick you when you hook the tugs,
and they like to run away."

And by golly, I was careful
as I worked 'em all that season.
I never did put down them lines.
Even when my hands were freezin'.

Then one day I tried my luck out,
'cuz I was runnin' late.
I left the lines upon the wagon,
and I talked 'em through the gate.

Well, they came through like seasoned troopers,
and they stopped at my command.
I guess they wanted me to think
I had the upper hand.

And that is how it went for weeks.
Them a foolin' me.
Me, thinkin' I'm the one on top.
Them waitin', don't you see.

Now the last load of my daily route,
was for the saddle cavvy.
And I was gettin' plumb proud of my bronco team.
They were gettin' pretty savvy.

Now I had opened up the gate.
Just spoke to Jude and Satan.
And they had barely tightened the tugs,
when the Earth began to shakin'.

'Cuz that cavvy came a foggin',
with their heads and tails up high.
A throwin' lots of snowballs
off their hooves up in the sky.

Well, ole Jude, he starts to lungin'.
And ole Satan sees the fun.
And I'm standin' pretty helpless.
And I'm feelin' pretty dumb.

I grab ole Satan's bridle,
as he breaks into a lope.
I'm prayin' that he'll give to me.
It is my only hope.

But by now, we've got some speed up,
and the Devil wants my soul.
So I pitch out next time I hit the ground.
And through the snow I roll.

A hopin' to get clear the wreck,
not tangled in the tack.
And I hope that loaded wagon
don't come screamin' up my back.

Them horses take a circle,
into the "catch corral."
And there some shortly after,
things begin to go to hell.

'Cuz the gate, it is quite narrow,
and the team don't come out straight.
And they leave 'bout half that wagon
just a hangin' in the gate.

Then they go to racin',
all around that split-rail lot.
And the harness and the wagon,
gettin' scattered. Damned if not!

And the corner of that wagon,
hits the corner of them rails.
And it surely sends 'em skyward,
'cuz they ain't put up with nails.

I could see that it would happen,
and I knew it'd be my fate.
When that team began to line up,
on that fancy "Ox Bow" gate.

Now it had real authentic ox bows,
and it was carved, and it was painted.
When the owner and the boss rode up,
I nearly almost fainted.

Well, the only thing would save it,
is if that ole team should stop.
So I waved my arms and hollered,
and in front of them I hopped.

Well, that team put on the binders,
and at last a breath I took.
When they finally got it halted,
then they just stood there and shook.

But the parts that still had pieces,
also had a lot of slack.
And that tongue came through the middle.
And it gave that gate a crack.

Well, it came a bustin' downward,
into match-wood, in a pile.
And I see the cow-boss start to look,
and I see him start to smile.

'Cuz he knew the work of Satan.
And he knew the work of Jude.
Like maybe he had been there,
and somehow he understood.

But it took a little longer
for the owner quite to see,
all the humor in the havoc
what had just befallen me.

But at last I got him grinnin'
when he asked and heard me say.
"Hell, there for just a second,
I thought they might get plumb away."

SANTA HELPS SHIP

We were shipping steers off the West Side. That's the name of the country that lays out west of Lakeview, OR. The boss owned an outfit out there, and that's were we ran our yearlings in the summer.

We had the corral behind the alley loaded with big steers, and we're bringing up what ever number of them that the truck driver calls out. There were about six or seven trucks there, and all of the drivers are standing on the cat-walk of the chute helping each other load.

There is one of these drivers that has particularly caught our eye. He's wearing a brand new pair of bright red coveralls and has a full white beard. It isn't long before we're calling him Santa Claus. He is the last truck to load. We've got about a half a load of odds and ends left, and the neigh-bor is going to finish it out. The neighbors aren't there with their cattle yet, so the rest of the trucks hit the road and take the steers somewhere closer to corn. Santa comes down the chute to visit while we wait.

The corral was built in such a way, that the barn served as one side of the alley leading up to the loading chute. All the time that Santa has been visiting, he has been standing in the chute, which has a plank floor. I guess he didn't notice that our horses were up to their knees in mud. It had been raining for about a week, and that alley would catch all of the run-off of the barn and could sure get sloppy. Finally the neighbors are all weighed up, brand inspected, and ready to load. Santa figures his load, calls out a number, and we bring 'em. He was going to panel these off on the top deck of the truck. There is one ole steer that's on the fight, and he puts Santa off the top deck before he can get the gate closed.

Down out of the truck in the wink of an eye,
for as old as he is, he's still pretty spry.
He zips down the chute like a kid half his age.
The steer's right behind him, a bellerin' rage.
With his tail in the air, that ole steer sure roared
Right out over Santa when he stepped off that board.
Now Santa is down, and his beard's full of goo,
And the tracks down his back, well, they're gooey, too.
Now the truck's finally loaded, and the steer, he's back in.
And Santa is goo from his boots to his chin.
As he drove off that night, we all heard him say
"I've had quite enough of a quite chitty day."

LEG HOLD TRAP

*This poem is based on a true story
that happened to Bill Hickey. Bill
spent four or five hours trapped,
wishing his arm would break so he
could get away. Finally, a neighbor
heard him hollering and rescued him.*

March has finally got here,
     and the song that's mostly sung,
says that calvin' is upon us,
     and that spring has finally sprung.

But is winter really over?
     Some nights would make me wonder.
With my hand around a spot-light,
     and my fingers gettin' number.

Them big, wet, snowflakes fallin',
     'till I can hardly see my way.
And I wish that it would quit it.
     I've got lots to do today.

But I put them thoughts on hold a while,
     'cuz it's still four hours 'till dawn.
And the heifer, I've been watchin',
     has convinced me, something's wrong.

So I gets her up real easy,
     and I heads her for the shed.
And I wonder, "Am I rushin' things?
     Or is the booger dead?"

When I gets her to the head-catch,
     her horns won't quite fit through.
So I slides a pole behind her.
     And I figure, that'll do

'till I can find just what's the problem.
     Then I'll tie her head up tight.
Then I'll slide that pole out of my road,
     so I can pull her right.

So I sheds my coat and rolls my sleeves,
    and takes a search by Braile.
I'm hopin' for two feet and nose.
    Anything but just a tail.

Aha, his two front feet are there.
    But where's his little head?
He seems to be a lookin',
    out the other end instead.

So I reach in deep, a searchin'.
    Hope to fish it back around.
When that heifer, backs into the pole,
    and promptly does go down.

Now I'm not really made for bendin',
    for what the situation calls.
And you can tell just when she's strainin',
    by the high pitch in my squalls.

I'd kick and scream and cuss her,
    but she's got that pole wedged tight.
Then I get to knowin'
    that I'm trapped there for the night.

Then I'd trade off on my cussin'.
    Sometimes I'd beg and plead.
Then I got to thinkin',
    I'll just whistle up my steed.

The Lone Ranger, he'd call Silver.
    Roy Rogers, he'd call Trigger.
That cribbin' S-O-B I ride,
    is just what I need, I figure.

I tried to "beaver" through it,
    but my dentures weren't in tight.
I tried to break it with my knees.
    I tried throughout the night.

But at last a rigs a comin'.
    It's my neighbor up for hay.
Sometimes he stops for coffee.
    And I sure hope he stops today.

I really get to yellin',
     as that pickup's gettin' near.
I'm hopin' that he's stoppin',
     and I'm prayin' that he hears.

At last the shed door opens,
     and he says, "You havin' fun?"
"I'm really in a pickle here.
     My arm has gone plumb numb."

Oh no, here comes the green stuff.
     All night, it's been a fear.
I only have two choices,
     so I takes it in the ear.

He kinda looks me over,
     and he says, "You look a fright.
It looks to me like you have spent
     a pretty, chitty night."

"Get up, ole girl, he's had enough."
     And damned if she don't stand.
I gets my arm out of her.
     It dangles like a rubber band.

I feel the blood rush down it,
     'till my finger-nails throb.
"You go on up there to the house.
     I'll finish this little job."

So I brewed us up some coffee.
     And to him I'd tip my cap.
'Cuz there's nothing sweet as neighbors,
     when you're in a leg-hold trap.

CAB-RIDE

It seems that when you gather a piece of country, the last animals to come off are a couple of old bachelor bulls. This is a story that I heard about loading some bulls, but I don't know who was involved or in what part of the country that it happened.

It seemed that the boys had gathered a couple of snuffy Brangus bulls and had them trapped for a moment in a falling down little wire lot. They knew that it wouldn't hold them for very long as these old bulls could jump about anything. They quickly backed up the stock trailer to the gate and bailed out to load the bulls. The pickup and trailer was about three feet away and parallel to the fence that served as a wing to the trap. As they jumped out, the guy on the passenger side left his door open and it almost touched the fence. They swung the trailer door open and ran around the outside of the lot, hoping that the bulls would jump right into the trailer.

The first bull stepped right in, but it rattled the trailer around a bit, and the trailer door came shut a little. The second bull, seeing an escape route, took a run for freedom. When he got to the passenger door of the pickup, there wasn't enough room to get by, so he tried his luck at crawling across the seat.

Now pickups these days are fairly roomy but weren't really designed to hold a full grown Brangus bull in the cab. The bull got in, but he was having trouble getting out. The boys finally had to open the driver side door and let the bull remodel the pickup as he crawled on out the other side. He broke out the windows and broke off the gear shift and the steering wheel, as he put bulges and creases wherever they were needed to accommodate his size.

How would you like to have to explain that one to the boss?

I'LL JUST NAME HIM COWBOY

I got this poem from a painting of Penny
Onstott's entitled "Takin' Off The Edge."

I've watched this ole bay colt for now on three years.
    He often don't mix with the bunch.
It's not that he's whipped-out or cranky.
    And if I'm a readin' my hunch,
he's gonna be mostly pure business,
    not longin' for pettin' and grain,
but noble and proud and upstanding.
    Behind that ole eye, there's a brain.
Oh, he plays when it's time to be playin'.
    He moves with incredible ease.
He don't get hisself in a corner.
    And when runnin', he sure splits the breeze.
But when playin's all through, he pulls off to himself.
    Not feelin' the need to be near.
The rest, they all hang there together,
    like they've all got something to fear.
But him, he's content to his lonesome.
    Don't need constant camaraderie.
So I think that I'll just name him "Cowboy",
    'cuz in a way, he's a whole lot like me.

A COYOTE FOX HUNT

*This poem is based on a true story. Tom
(T) Anderson and I were working for
Lynch's and gathering cattle off of the
forest permit east of Lakeview, OR.*

Now me and "T" was ridin',
for the outfit, double J.
And both of us were full of youth,
and both were full of play.

And we'd been seein' lots of coyote pups,
and they were gettin' prime.
So we thought that we might skin a few,
and maybe make a dime.

So we started packin' pistols
as we gathered in them hills.
And we were countin' money
from our unclaimed coyote kills.

And the boss had seen us leavin'
with our pistols hangin' free.
So he stopped us, just to set things straight,
and school on me and "T".

"Now back in County Cork," says he,
"We did this just for fun.
We chased the fox a horseback.
And we didn't pack a gun.

"We did it for the hounds and chase,
but mostly for the thrills.
'Cuz when you get thirty 'jumpers,' lads,
you're bound to see some spills.

"So remember, when you're out there,
jump the hedges, then the ditches.
And it's 'tally ho the fox', boys.
Not, 'there goes the red tailed Sunday britches.'"

And we were glad he set us straight,
'cuz later in the day,
we had a coyote, "fox hunt,"
and we knew the proper way.

Now, up in Summit Prairie,
'bout half mile from any tree,
sat this silly, dumb coyote,
just watchin' me and "T."

We rode within about fifty yards,
and we were feelin' wise.
"You get off. I'll hold your horse.
You give him the surprise."

"T" pulled right down on him
and took his deadly aim.
He meant to hit him in the head,
but only bent his frame.

Well, he took off a runnin'.
packin' one, and usin' three.
Tommy emptied out his pistol,
then he sorta looked at me.

I handed him my pistol
and said, "Here, get him while you're hot."
And he emptied out my pistol,
but he missed with every shot.

Then Tommy quickly mounted,
and the huntsman's bugle blew.
We raced across the meadow.
"Tah doo." "Tah doo." "Tah doo."

Just before we hit them quakey trees,
I said, "Tommy, this is it.
Just like chasin' foxes."
Lots of downfalls. Holy Shit!

I hit a tree,
and it knocked me to the clover.
By the time I got back on my horse,
for me the hunt was over.

I knew that it was over.
I didn't even know which way.
Then I heard ole Tom a barkin'.
Mister Coyote was at bay.

By the time I finally got there,
here sits Tom upon this log.
A loadin' up his pistol,
and a barkin' like a dog.

"I thought you'd never get here.
This barkin' is hard work.
You look a little dirty.
You been rollin' in the dirt?"

I smiled and tried to pass it off.
"Did the coyote get away?"
"No, he's burrowed in this hollow log,
but he won't come out and play."

We observed the situation.
Tom's solution came real quick.
"I'll cover with both pistols,
you go in and poke him with a stick."

And he said it was my duty,
and at duties I don't shirk.
'Cuz he'd been doin' all the barkin',
all the chasin', all the work.

And I couldn't hardly argue,
my end had been some slack.
So I breaks me off a tree limb,
and proceeds with the attack.

Now I'm inchin' down this hollow log,
which, by the way, was dark.
When I hear this muffled growlin',
and I hear a muffled bark.

"Is that you, "T"?" I kind of asked.
I heard him echo, "Pull."
So I poked that muffled growler,
And, boy, did he unsull.

He came out o'er the top of me
like a banshee in the night.
Like a screamin' herd of clawmarks.
Like a rocket takin' flight.

He hit the end of that tunnel,
and, boy, was he a runnin'.
And Tommy opened up on him.
And, boy, was he a gunnin'.

Well, it might be in the water.
or it might be in the air.
But, Tommy emptied out both pistols,
and he never touched a hair.

So once more we are a horseback.
Once more we sound the horn.
Tommy's lookin' pretty good,
but I'm bloody, scratched, and torn.

Then that silly coyote,
heads back out across the grass.
And we put up both our pistols,
'cuz we couldn't hit our ass.

Then we jerked our ropes down,
and make a quick, small, loop.
Tommy makes the head catch,
and I finally make the scoop.

Well, we didn't "Tally Ho" him,
but we put him to the test.
Maybe not by "Robert's Rules of Order,"
but that's how it's done out West.

SNAKE BIT

Ray Padgett was putting up the hay for Henry O'Keefe one year and tells this story:

"It was almost dark, when the conditioner on the swather plugged up again for the hundredth time that day. I'd had enough of it for a day, so I just went home without cuttin' that hay out of the conditioner. Just figured on getting it in the morning.

"Early the next day, me and my little girl goes out to Adel to get at it. We killed two big rattle snakes on the way to work. If there is one thing in this world that I don't like it's a damned old snake, especially a rattler. When we got to the swather, I crawled in under it on my back and started cuttin' that hay off that conditioner. Ellen looks under there and tells me, 'Dad? I don't know how to tell you this with out spookin' you, but there's a great big old snake, coiled up right above your head on that shield.'

"That was plenty enough said, so I banged my head on that conditioner just for to start the race, and then set a hundred yard dash record on my hocks and elbows.

"Later that day, Henry comes by and wants to show me where to swath out a hay corral. I've settled down some, but I'm still pretty snakey. As we're walkin' out through the tall grass in that stackyard, I stepped on a piece of barbed wire that was about a foot long. As I stepped on one end of it, the other end came up and struck my leg and hung up there. It's a terrible thing to do to yourself, but when I got done kickin' my shins black and blue, I took my foot and just scraped that ole barbed wire right down my leg. To say the least, I went home pretty well scratched up, and it was all self-inflicted."

AND THE WIND BEGINS TO BLOW

The wind is howlin', howlin',
And it makes an eerie sound.
And the snow is blowin, blowin'.
But it doesn't touch the ground.

It rained clear up 'till lunch time.
Then the temperature dropped down.
Now the wind is howlin', howlin',
And the snow don't touch the ground.

We're wet from mornin' ridin'.
Snow pelts us in the face.
But, we're trottin', trottin' homeward,
at a fightin', drivin' pace.

Can't hardly stand to face it
as we ride into the wind.
Horse's necks are bowin', bowin',
as we face our medicine.

Our hands are numbin', numbin',
as we trot against the blast.
The cold is strong against us.
And the distance, it seems vast.

Our eyes are stingin', stingin',
as we try to see our way.
Horses' necks and breath is steamin',
as we trot on through the day.

Makes it hard for breathin', breathin'.
Our coats are cold and damp.
But we're trottin', trottin' onwards
to the comforts of our camp.

The snow is pilin', pilin',
on the one side of our hat.
And I hate to even look up,
for to see just where we're at.

But at last, we finally make it.
Horses stoppin' at the shack.
Our feet are breakin', breakin'
as we slide out of our kack.

Our feet are nonrespondin',
as we strip our mounts of saddle.
Been ten miles of poundin' snowflakes,
since we dropped that bunch of cattle.

Cold fingers fumble, fumble
for to get the throatlatch free.
Horses spittin' bridles,
as at last, they are set free.

Men are cold and cursin',
as we put away our tack.
Then we head 'er to the bunkhouse,
and we're glad that we are back.

Fire crackin', crackin',
as we stroke it with a poker.
Water's boilin', boilin'
as with wood we stoke her.

Coffee sippin', sippin',
with cold hands around warm cups.
Bodies shiver, shiver,
thawin' out and warmin' up.

On about the third cup,
the stories get to flowin'.
And the wind is howlin', howlin',
And the snow is blowin', blowin'.

Then Ed, he starts to grinnin',
and he says, "Do you remember,
the fall of '67,
when we gathered in the timber?"

"Now that there was a storm, boys.
This'n ain't too much at all.
In fact, compared to that one,
this ain't nothin' but a squall."

And everyone remembered one,
to put this one below.
Then an eerie kind of silence.
As the wind begins to BLOW!

197

TIMMY GETS TIRED

Back when a cowboy is young, there isn't anything that he won't ride. Every cow or bull that gets roped and doctored always seems to come up with a passenger.

If there was ever any cows in the corral after dinner, they really caught it. Strays or the bosses, it didn't much matter. We could get them into a chute and get a rope on them there.

That summer, we came in off the desert with a "slick" yearling bull. We'd branded and castrated him earlier that summer, but it hadn't changed his attitude much. He was still on the fight. After dinner, we went down to ride him.

Timmy had won the coin toss and was going to be the one that got to give him the first test drive. The rest of us would be bull fighters. This ole yearlin' didn't buck much, but Timmy was having a good time just sitting their chasin' us around. We'd run around him, and that steer would take right to us. We had some old tractor tires cut in half that we used to grain the horses in. I was standin' in the middle of the corral with one of these tires standing upright. By this time, Timmy is sitting on the beast backwards, using his tail for a bronc rein. That ole steer took a run at me and crawled right through that tire. He sure didn't take into account his extra passenger, and Timmy really got shucked out. Timmy couldn't figure out what had happened, and we were all laughin' too hard to tell him.

THE TEAM

*I was traveling home late one night
and turned onto the last thirty miles
of gravel road towards Plush. It was
snowing hard, and the road was
drifting. I was wondering if I should
stay on the oil and take the long
way home, when the words of Tom
Anderson came to me. "Where's
your pioneer spirit? Think they
turned back just because they hit a
little snow drift?"*

*As I broke those drifts across that
cut-off I got to thinking of my
grandparents. How they had
followed a team of horses to
Colorado and homesteaded. How
they had been married and pulling
together for 76 years. And of my own
parents, how many times when the
road of life got a little bit muddly,
they made it by pulling together. I
stopped and wrote "The Team."*

All my life, with even tugs,
    they've leaned into the collar.
You always picked up the lines and spoke.
    You never whipped and hollered.
You treated them with due respect.
    They gave it back ten-fold.
It seems the tougher that things got,
    the harder that team pulled.
I've seen 'em bust them chest high drifts
    and pull high water too.
And if you cared to watch and learn,
    they'd teach some things to you.
I've seen 'em inches off the ground
    and sway to get one started.
And I have been responsible
    for some heavy loads they've carted.
For fifty years—been side by side,
    one's never left the other.
So, please, God, take in open hand,
    my father, and my mother.

GLOSSARY

bag . . . . a cow's udder.

bedded down . . . . bucked off.

big titted cow . . . . a cow whose teats get too large for a calf to nurse.

bloat . . . . Alfalfa, though it is a great feed, in excess or with the wrong conditions, puts off a gas which is toxic. A cow that is bloated severely gets so much pressure on its diaphram that it can't breathe.

blow the cork . . . . to buck.

breaks out late . . . . getting a late start as in horse racing and roping events.

bringing up the field . . . . last in a race.

broncs . . . . untrained or cranky horses.

brushed up . . . . hiding in thick brush.

buckaroo . . . . a cowboy/derived from the Spanish vacquero. Usually associated with cowboys in the Great Basin Area or California.

bump a bucking horse . . . . running into a horse with your own to knock him off balance and make it quit bucking.

bury his hocks . . . . slide to a stop.

butcher cow pen . . . . a pen at an auction yard which holds usually older cows going to the packing plant to be processed into hamburger.

cahones . . . . testicles.

calve . . . . when a cow gives birth to a baby calf.

canned . . . . fired.

catch corral . . . . a corral where horses are caught.

Cavvy . . . . a group of saddle horses.

Chowchilla rowels . . . . very large and sharp Mexican spurs.

Cinderella Strap . . . . or stampede string/a string on a hat that is placed under your chin to keep your hat from falling off.

collar . . . . that part of a harness that fits around the horse's neck.

cribber . . . . a horse that eats on wood, corrals, barns, etc.

dallies . . . . turns taken around a saddle horn to hold something that has been roped.

dees . . . . the "D" rings in your saddle that your cinch is attached to. If a person is in the dees during a bucking horse ride, he is not spurring.

dehorn . . . . to surgically remove horns.

Drag or drags . . . . the tail end of a trail drive, riding drag or bringing up the stragglers.

dregs . . . . bottom of a container of liquid, coffee grounds, etc.

dry lot . . . .livestock pen without water.

first calf heifer . . . . a young cow having her first calf.

flankin' calves . . . . As a calf is dragged to the branding fire, the people working on the ground grab the rope in one hand and the calf's flank with the other. They then lift them off balance and plop them on their side.

foot-rope . . . . a long soft cotton rope used to tie up a foot.

forked . . . . a good bronc rider.

free verse . . . . poems that don't rhyme. Known in cowboy terms as "open range" poems.

fresh horse . . . . a horse that hasn't been ridden lately, a rested horse.

fringe . . . . in this case, one's hair.

green . . . . inexperienced.

green colt . . . . a young inexperienced horse.

Greenhorn Irishman . . . . an immigrant from Ireland who has just arrived in this country.

hand . . . . a good cowboy, one who understands his business.

head catch . . . . front end of a chute / stanchion.

heavy cow . . . . a cow that is full term with a calf.

heavy handed . . . . a person who is always jerking and pulling too hard on the bit.

hobbles . . . . a short strap of leather, rope, or chain that secures the feet of horses so they can't travel.

hogans . . . . Indian homes.

homesteads . . . . places where a feller has been bucked off.

honky tonk . . . . bar or saloon.

hoorahed . . . . laughed at or made fun of.

horses with legs . . . . a horse that travels well. A legged-up horse is one that is in shape.

in a storm . . . . out of control.

inside cattle . . . . cattle around the ranch in pastures.

kack . . . . saddle.

light hand . . . . a good horseman is light handed, meaning he does not use excessive force on the bit.

mantie . . . . a piece of canvas about 8 feet square that whatever you are hauling is placed in. It is then folded up much like a package, then lashed to the packsaddle.

mecate . . . . a rope coming from your headstall or bosal to your belt, usually part of your rein setup, oftentimes made of horse hair.

mother up . . . . letting the cows find their calves after they have been separated in a herd or trail drive.

Nosler's kiss . . . . putting something out of its misery by shooting it. Nosler is a make of bullet.

out of horse . . . . a tired horse.

outfit . . . . ranch.

outside cattle . . . . cattle on the range.

Oxbow . . . . the name of a ranch in Prairie City, OR / a wooden collar for a team of oxen.

pair . . . . a cow and her calf.

preconditioned . . . . calves having all their calfhood shots before weaning.

pull a snaffle bit . . . . the pull and release used on a snaffle bit.

pulled the pin . . . . going to move, derived from pulling a picket pin.

puss . . . . face.

reps . . . . a person acting as a representative of a ranch.

roan . . . . a hair color. Red and white would make a red roan, black and white makes a blue roan.

rodeer . . . . holding a group of cattle without the aid of fences.

romals . . . . the end piece of a set of bridle reins that acts as a quirt.

rowels . . . . the round star shaped disc at the end of a spur.

run back . . . . When cows and calves get separated, they will go back to the place where the calf last nursed.

savvy . . . . to understand.

scooped up the pair . . . . roping both hind feet.

scratch him a little . . . . to spur.

singles cattle . . . . cattle that are run through a sale ring one at a time. Maybe something not uniform enough to go through as a pen lot (group).

slick . . . . unbranded.

snaffle bit . . . . a bit used mostly on young horses still being trained, pulling a young horse's head aroung to get it to turn, versus neck reining, where an older more well trained horse will turn by simple pressure on the neck from the reins.

snide . . . . a horse of inferior qualities.

sours . . . . sourdough.

spreads . . . . ranches.

sticking a bloated cow . . . . poking a knife into the paunch of a cow to let excess gas escape.

string . . . . a group of horses, usually 4 to 10 that a particular person is riding. A cavvy is made up of each rider's string of horses.

stuffer . . . . a taxidermist.

sun fishing . . . . a move made by a bucking animal where all four legs are to one side in the middle of a jump.

synchronization . . . . An Artificial Insemination Technician can't spend a whole estrus cycle at one outfit, so they do what is called synchronization by placing a little hormone implant in the cow's ear, which brings them all into estrus in a short period of time.

tack . . . . gear, saddle, bridle, etc.

tagging . . . . a tag placed on the back of cattle at the auction yard to identify ownership.

tapped off . . . . in rhythm with a bucking horse.

trap . . . . small corral.

tugs . . . . that part of a harness that attaches the horse to the wagon.

twine . . . . lariat rope.

twisted . . . . rode.

wanna-bes . . . . people who dress like and try to act like cowboys.

warbles . . . . a grub that surfaces on the backs of livestock.

wild rag . . . . a neck scarf.

winning spot . . . . first in a race.

wrangle . . . . to gather a bunch of saddle horses to catch the mounts for the day. Sometimes known as jingling.